D1823820

Becoming!

A Lifetime of Prose

A Lifetime of Prose

Bob E. McGlothlin

Copyright © 2018 by Bob E. McGlothlin

All rights reserved. This book or any portion thereof may not be reproduced or transmitted in any form or manner, electronic or mechanical, including photocopying, recording, or by any information storage or retrieval system, without the express written permission of the copyright owner except for the use of brief quotations in a book review or other noncommercial uses permitted by copyright law.

Printed in the United States of America

Library of Congress Control Number:		2018949932
ISBN:	Softcover	978-1-64376-039-1
	eBook	978-1-64376-040-7

Republished by: PageTurmer, Press and Media LLC

Publication Date: 08/13/2018

To order copies of this book, contact:

PageTurner, Press and Media
601 E., Palomar St., Suite C-478, Chula Vista, CA 91911
Phone: 1-888-447-9651
Fax: 1-619-632-6328
Email: order@pageturner.us
www.pageturner.us

Contents

U's

V's

W's

Becoming!

A piece of canvas becomes a work of art
Once the artist makes his final mark.
A piece of stone becomes a sculpture
Once the sculptor chips away the last chip.
For a poet,
A plain piece of paper becomes a priceless gem
Once he finally lifts his pen.
God is the artist
That's painting beauty within the heart of our soul.
God is the sculptor
That's chipping away at the flaws in our character
To make us into His perfect image.
God is the poet
That would turn the plainness of our lives
Into poetic praise.

Contained within this volume are words of prose
that were written while in the process of becoming.
(ORGANIZED ALPHABETICALLY BY TITLE)

FROM THE POET'S PEN

Dear reader:

It is my sincere prayer and desire that God will use these words of prose to inspire and encourage you to view life from a completely different perspective than what you are used to. You see, so many of us go through life experiencing difficulties, trials, tests, temptations, and troubles of all kinds; and, many times, we only focus on the negative aspects of each situation. When we do this, it makes it so very hard for us to see God's light in the midst of all the darkness around us. It also makes it hard for us to understand God's wisdom and purpose in allowing us to go through each situation; unless, of course, we can find enough grace to change our focus. So, I hope that God will use these words to encourage someone to look beyond the way things appear; and at least seek to view life's situations as God sees them. As you prayerfully read the following pages, may you receive an impartation of God's grace and power to overcome in the midst of the troubles of your life.

Sincerely,
Poet and Author:
Bob E. McGlothlin

A's

A Delicate Matter

Behold how
Delicate a matter
When hope grows on
An illusive platter;
To destroy the illusion
Would throw the soul
Into much confusion.
In order to save the soul
From hopeless despair
One needs to
Scrape the platter
With tender loving care.
Then when hope
Is fully resting
On a solid plane;
The illusion can be broken
With just a little pain.

Then when the pain subsides
And peace returns again;
Hope can still grow
On solid ground within.

A Diamond In The Rough

Sometimes we feel like
Our life is as black
As a piece of coal,
And that the pressures of this life
Are getting pretty intense;
But consider what it actually takes
To turn a piece of coal
Into a diamond;
For a piece of coal
Is actually a diamond
In the rough;
For once sufficient pressure is applied
For a sufficient amount of time,
Then a diamond is formed.

A God Of Detail

God is not only so big that He created a galaxy, but He is also a God of great detail throughout all of His creation. He paid enough attention to each intricate part of creation to give it specific design and detail. For example: the leaf structure of every kind of tree is different from every other kind of tree; and although each individual leaf of a particular tree is similar enough to identify it as a leaf of that kind of tree, it is individual enough that it can stand alone. No other leaf is exactly like it. That speaks of a God of detail. Family members favor each other, but each person is an individual in character, personality, and looks. Just consider the awesomeness of universe after universe, all of which is held together by unseen gravitational forces. Then consider the tiny ant colony, and the order in which they conduct themselves. Consider humanity that wouldn't be able to survive the depths of the sea. Yet some of our scientists tell us that they've discovered some varieties of fish that live there that would actually explode if they were brought close enough to the surface. Now, that *speaks of a God of detail. Oh, how awesome is our God who is not only big enough to have created galaxy after galaxy, but is also concerned enough to pay attention to the details of life on any particular level.*

A Good Place To Pray

Most of us pray
At a church altar
Or by a pew
Not really considering
If any place else will do.
Some people pray
At home by their bedside
Or possibly in a closet
Or some other place to hide.
Other people pray
In a hospital or a jail
In a quiet tone
Or possibly a yell.
Some people pray
While walking in a field
Or on a wooded trail
Is where to God they yield.

But whether you pray
At a church altar or pew
Or maybe by your bedside,
Closet, or hospital room,

Any of these places
Will do any day
For each of them are
A good place to pray;
For it doesn't matter if you
Are in a field,
Or in a jail,
On an open street
Or a wooded trail.
Any of these places
Will do any day,
For each one of them are
A good place to pray.

A Good Time To Pray

When you're living your life
Behind closed doors,
And you're hungry for light,
And ready for war;
When you want to revolt
Against your own ways;
This is a good time
To kneel down and pray.

When your life is a mess,
And all out of sorts;
And you're getting really tired
Of the enemy's darts;
And you're not really sure
To him what to say;
This is a good time
To kneel down and pray.

When you're looking for answers,
And are finding none;
And your life has ceased
To be any fun;

To find peace of mind,
You can't find the way;
This is a good time
To kneel down and pray.

When all is in order,
And nothing's amiss;
Everything's going right,
Your life is in bliss,
And blessings just cross
Your path day to day;
This is a good time
To kneel down and pray;

For we never know what
The future may hold;
Or what's coming up
Just down the road.
Around the next curve
Something might say,
"You'd better take time
To kneel down and pray."

A Hand

If you've lost
Someone you love,
Just look to God,
Who is above;
For He's bending down
With outstretched hand,
Reaching for
The broken man.
A hand to heal
He does possess;
So, why don't you put
Him to the test?

If you've lost
Your way down here,
Just look to God;
For He's always near
To shine His light
Upon your path;
And steer you round
Ole Satan's wrath.
A hand to guide

He does possess;
So, why don't you put
Him to the test?

If you've lost
Your peace of mind,
Just look to God;
For He'll help you find
The way to peace
Through His powerful Cross,
And help you recover
Just what you've lost.
A hand to restore
He does possess;
So, why don't you put
Him to the test?

If you've lost A heart to live,
Just look to God;
For new life He gives.
He'll help you mend
That broken heart;
And show you a new
Place you can start.

A hand to renew
He does possess;
So, why don't you put
Him to the test?

A Real Winner

A real winner
Is considerate,
And is kind,
And for the most part,
Has others in mind.
Sometimes when someone appears
To be a winner in life;
They are really losers
When it comes to coping with strife.
Real winners may not be
Rich in fortune or in fame;
But real winners know how to
Call upon Jesus name.

★ ★ ★

A Request

Lord, If I cannot marry
And have myself a family;
Or possibly a ministry
That would affect the lives
Of souls that are many;
Is there yet a purpose
In my remaining here,
Struggling to keep on living,
Striving just to make it down here?
Now, Lord, I'm not saying
That'll take my own life;
For that, in itself,
Will be nothing more
Than vanity or strife.
But, Lord, this is my request
At nearly forty-five;
Either use me as a husband
And a father real soon alive;
Or make my life fruitful, oh Lord,
In both word and deed;

By affecting the lives of others
Who through my word they'll heed;
Or just prepare me, oh Lord,
For the end of this my life;
And take me home to be with You;
And end all of this strife.

A Silent Witness

There was a silent witness,
One that never spoke a word;
But lived a life of righteousness
That couldn't help, but to be heard;
For this life that walked so straight,
And never stepped off the path
Shone so bright and radiant
That it revealed the coming wrath
To all those that were around him
That failed to walk so straight.
It also revealed God's mercy,
The path leading to those Pearly Gates.
Many felt conviction,
And turned from a life of sin.
Others continued on,
Resenting the word they'd seen.

There was a silent witness,
One that never spoke a word;
But lived a life of faithfulness
That many a life was stirred.
These could not help but see

Their need for God above,
And because of this silent witness
Sought for God's Holy love.
So, if you're a silent witness,
One that never speaks a word;
Continue on in faithfulness;
So, that your message is heard.
You never know who's watching;
Or how they're affected by
Your Holy consecration,
And your faithful eye.

A Testimony

All through school
I sought one thing
To be accepted
By the status-quo;
But did not find
That blessed thing;
But tried really hard although.
I got into fights,
Not once or twice,
But nearly every day.
Twas no fun,
Almost never won.
As for them
It was just play.
Whenever we'd move,
It would repeat
Just as it was before.
It got to where
When I'd come home
I didn't want to
Go back there anymore.
No one knows

The pain I'd feel
Day out and day in.
Just the longing
That I would have
For just one
Lifelong friend.
Then one day
When I was ten
I met this neighbor girl.
All summer long
Our friendship grew
'Til her parents' plan unfurled.
She moved away.
I painfully stayed
Wondering why
This had to be.
Until I got down
In my backyard
Down on my bended knee.
When I asked God
To fix it all,
This thing He did for me.
He took the pain
Out of my heart;
From it set me free.
Before this time
I had not known
If there really was a God.

But since that day
Unto this one
In pursuit of Him
Have I trod.

Although when I
Was only ten
I did not know His name;
I asked my parents
Where I should start;
"We're Baptist," they proclaimed.
I don't remember
But just once
That we'd ever
Been to church.
But I decided
I had to know;
So I began my search.
Then at eleven
Is when we moved
To the country
Out on a farm,
Just walking distance
From a Baptist Church;
To go would do no harm.
For the next six years,
Went faithfully,
Wednesday, Sunday morning and night.
Learned a lot Of God's Word,

To which I had no light.
At seventeen
When I saw

A deacon curse and swear;
I got caught up
In judging him,
And fell prey
To Satan's snare.
The next four years
I started running around
With the wrong crowd.
Drinking, carousing,
And doing things
Of which I'm not too proud.
During this time,
Just like ole Jonah,
I ran off
To another land.
Only to find
That God was there
Reaching for me
With His hand.
Again I prayed
On a hillside
Not ready to give in;
But God was patient
And so kind;
And faithful to the end.

Back in the States
He came again;
And called me

By my name.
Could not resist
His audible voice;
So I turned to
Him once again.
This time I knew
Beyond a doubt
His presence is so real;
And His hand
Was on my life,
For His Spirit
I could sure feel.
Again I went
To a Baptist Church;
For this was all I knew;
But soon God brought
Some witnesses
To show me
What was true.
First a man
From the Church of Christ
Showed me Acts 2:38;
And said I must
Be baptized right
If I want to see

Those pearly gates;
But when I asked
Of the other part,
About this Holy Ghost,
He said it was
Not for today;
Then I felt,
This must be a hoax.
Two weeks past;
And I met a man
From the Assembly of God;
Who told me
I needed The Holy Ghost
To help me Through life trod.
But when I asked him
About Baptism,
He said all ways
Are the same;
So I decided
To wait until
More revelation came.
One year went by;
Then almost two;
And I had returned back home;
Saw God do things
In my life
That could only have
Come from His throne.

So again I looked
At the book of Acts

Chapter two, verse thirty-eight.
Asked God again
To reveal the truth.
This time it really came.
This time as I
Research His Word,
I met people
Both left and right
That had obeyed
This awesome truth;
And now stood there
As a light.
So I obeyed
This Word of truth
Found in Acts two,
Verse thirty-eight;
And found a friend
That would stand by me
All the way to
Those pearly gates.

A Tribute To The Manguns

Fifty years;
What were they like?
One of World War Two's
Aerial strikes?
Fighting principalities and powers
Through the power of prayer;
Building this Church
With tremendous care;
Carrying other's burdens
Upon their spiritual backs;
Until one day in Eternity
Their rewards will be stacked;
Caring for people
From dawn until dusk;
And sometimes at midnight,
They felt like they must.
Through prayer and the Word
They fought day and night
To build this Great Church
With Eternity in sight.
Fifty years of Marriage
And Ministry here

*Can only get
Angelic attention this year.*

*Fifty years;
What were they like?
One of World War Two's
Aerial strikes.
Written in honor of Bishop G. A. and Vesta Mangun on their
Fiftieth Wedding Anniversary*

A Wish

A wish is a desire,
Whether spoken or not;
And usually finds its source
Down deep within the heart.
It's manifested in longing;
And can be seen in the eyes
Of the longing soul,
Which cannot be disguised.
Oft times a wish is spoken,
And directed to a star;
And heard by angelic hosts
Listening from afar;
But whether a wish is spoken,
Or whether it is not,
God is the one who listens
To the longing heart.

Abiding in Christ

Abiding in Christ
Is rich and sweet
Once you've endured the pruning.
Abiding in Christ
Cannot be beat
Once submitted to the calling.
Pruning is painful
And submission is costly.
Self-denial's the path
That will bring you through
And set you free.
Abiding in Christ
Will bring you life
And help you endure
All the strife.

Accepted

To never be invited
As a guest to dinner,
Always the last one chosen
For a sporting team,
To be the object of
Every bully's scorn,
To be included is
Just a dream.
Isolated from my
Scholastic peers,
Not accepted by
The status-quo,
To just be asked
To tag along,
To soothe some pain
Or end some woe;
Living this life
So, all alone,
Without one close
Confiding friend,
Can be a painful
Road to trod

*If left alone
'Til the end.*

*But though man
May me
Not include,
And always leave me
'Til the last;
There is one thing
That I'm assured,
In God's Kingdom
The last is first,
And the first is last.
And though rejected
By peers quite oft,
And my opinion not
In this world respected,
There is one thing
Helps me endure;
In the beloved
I am accepted.*

Adversity

Adversity, adversity;
So you find yourself in adversity.
Perhaps if you knew
What's just beyond you,
It might help you through
This adversity;
For lessons are learned through adversity;
And honor is earned through adversity.
Sins are shunned through adversity;
And battles are won through adversity.
Plans are set through adversity;
And needs are met through adversity.
Visions are caught through adversity;
And lessons are taught through adversity.
Warnings we heed through adversity;
And successful men proceed through adversity.
Spirits are worn through adversity;
But nations were born through adversity.

So what is adversity;
But a blessing in disguise;
Sent to make you strong;
Intended to make you wise.

Adversity:
An unprecedented opportunity
To exercise your faith.

America, Let's Bless God

Although, through the years
Since this nation began,
God has blessed America;
For it was part of His plan
To utilize this nation
For the common good
To evangelize this world
With His Gospel understood;
But o'er the past few decades
This nation has been drifting
Away from His principles,
Away from His Holy ways.
Since September eleventh,
This tragedy so great
Where many lost their lives
As if in a quake,
Many are returning,
Yes, they are coming back
To the Cross of Calvary
To receive what they've lacked.
They're praying again as always
What the song did clearly say,

"God Bless America",
And deliver us today;

But it's time for all to see,
As through this day we trod,
It's time for old America
To finally bless God.

Among The Walking Dead

Living your life
Among the dead,
Whose sinful ways
You hold in dread;
For those that walk
In trespass and sin
Walk contrary to
Those born again.
Searching each day
For the life giving flow
That'll take you along
To an eternal goal;
For those who follow
Where this flow leads
Find a cleansing
Where a Savior bleeds.
It's hard to live life
Among those who are dead
In trespass and sin
Whose ways you so dread;
Unless you've placed
Your flesh on a cross,

And buried your sin
For their eternal loss,
And gained the right
New life to win
Once you've given your life over,
And been born again;
For without this experience
Of Christ's death where He bled,
And without the resurrection
You're walking in death;
And of you, my friend,
It can really be said,
You're daily among
The walking dead.

An Artist Dilemma

An artist pondering,
"Just what should I draw;
Mountains, valleys,
Hills, or falls;
Trees, flowers,
Rivers, or streams;
People that are kind,
Or angry and mean;
Clouds, rainbows,
Fog that is thick;
A holiday scene
With good ole Saint Nick?
Oh how can I express
What I'm feeling today;
Draw an empty street;
Or maybe a parade?"

While pondering there
A thought crossed his mind;
Then in just a moment
He fell asleep for a time.
Then began he to dream

Of a time and a place;
That no one had seen;
Or been in that case.

He dreamed of a room,
All colorful and bright.
He then saw himself standing
In a bright and shining light.
Then as he looked closer
At himself standing there;
He saw several spots
That seemed covered with hair.
As curiously he looked,
And pondered some more;
He then saw a man
In the shape of a door.

"Just what are these spots
That I'm covered with?"
Asking the door,
He said, "What is this?"

"These spots are your sins
The light has revealed.
While you were in darkness,
They were merely concealed."

"What should I do
To be rid of these spots?
Should I see a surgeon;

And have him cut me a lot?"

"That's not the answer,"
The door said to him.
"You must first be sorry
For all of these sins.
Then walk on closer,
And step right through me;
And you'll find yourself
All clean and spot free."

Then with a cry,
He showed his remorse;
And then to the door
He established his course.
Then as he looked down
To grab hold of the knob;
He saw just a name;
And started to sob.

"How do I open
This door to get in?
Please tell me so I
Can be rid of my sin."

"Just call out that name;
And step right on through;
For that name is what will
Open the door for you."

So then he cried "Jesus;"
And stepped right on in;
And found himself clean;
Set free from his sin.

Then he awoke;
And found he did know
About what to draw;
And which way he should go.

An Oasis In The Desert Of Life

All churches should become an oasis in the desert of life; for the Church of the Living God is supposed to be where the springs of living water come together to flow out. So, as you offer yourself up to the Living God in worshipful adoration and praise, open up your heart and allow the fountain of living water to erupt within you to cause the Spirit of God to flow through you into the Sanctuary. This is how the Spirit of God can effectively move upon a sinner's heart, through the spontaneous eruption of praise and worship that invokes the outpouring of Holy Ghost conviction to draw that sinner's soul unto Him, the fountain of living water. In Jesus Christ's own words, "He that believeth on me as the Scripture hath said, out of his belly shall flow rivers of living water." What is it that causes these rivers to flow? It is a belief that erupts into thanksgiving which will lead into heart-felt praises that in turn transforms spontaneously into worship. For once you actually believe in Jesus Christ "as the Scripture hath said," then you cannot help but to become thankful for the hope of eternal life in Him. A truly thankful heart can't help but praise the God of all the ages. And since "God inhabits the praises of His people," true heart-felt praise can only draw the soul into worshipful adoration of the Almighty God. Lost men should be able to taste of the living water as soon as they come into contact with the Body of Christ, whether it is the local church or just one or two members of the Body. The springs of living water should be flowing through you continually, as you go through your day. Sinners that you come into contact with should have their appetite for the things of God provoked to hunger. They should feel the life-giver flowing from you, wooing them into longing for what you have. If those springs are not flowing from you, you should desire to find out why. You should seek to find out what it is that is clogging up the well-spring of life within you. Commit yourself to a season of fasting and prayer to unclog the well-spring of your soul so that those springs can flow once again. The lost members of your families cannot "taste and see that the Lord is good" if your well is clogged. The people you work with cannot "taste and see that the Lord is good" unless your well is flowing, unless the Spirit is actually moving within your soul. Is the living water of the Spirit flowing through you? If not, then "it is time to seek the Lord, until He comes and rains righteousness upon you," until you have unclogged the well-spring of life within you, until you become a vital part of this oasis in the desert of life.

Angel Business

Angels coming.
Angels going.
All along to us unknowing.
Here to guide.
Here to direct,
And reveal to us
The Christian sect;
Showing us
The path to take
So that we
Then can escape
The coming trials
And coming tests
That will fall
Upon the rest.
Angels standing.
Angels fighting.
All the while,
We are guided
By the movement
Of these spirits,
Even though

We fail to hear it.
Angels bowing.
Angels flying.
In great reverence
They are crying
Holy, holy,
Holy is He
That has come
With great victory.
When angels come,
When angels go,
Whether or not
We ever know,
They are about
The Father's will,
And for us
They won't be still;
But they will stand,
And they will fight
For our salvation
Both day and night.

Angelic Protection

"He shall give His angels charge over thee, to keep thee in all thy ways" Psalm 91:11

I used to think
This verse applied
To only times
When His will I'd find.
But looking back
Ore my life
I've come to believe
It is not only of that kind;
For many times where I
Was kept by angelic hosts
Wasn't when I was on
The victory road;
But were those times
When I've wondered
Down my own path
Were times when angels
kept me from satanic wrath.

Angels

"A" is for the AWESOME
Presence that you feel.

"N" is for that NO ONE
Really comprehends their zeal.

"G" is for the GOD
Whom they serve both day and night.

"E" is for the ETERNAL REALM
In which they always fight.

"L" is for the LOVE OF GOD
Which motivates their work.

"S" is for the SALVATION OF MAN
For which they stay alert.

The BIBLE calls them ministers;
A flaming fire of God
Sent to help the heirs
Of the salvation of God;
We refer to them as ANGELS;
And often fail to see
That they are working day and night
To help and set us free.

Ariel

Ariel is so sweet,
Yes, Ariel is nice.
It seems like she's made
Of sugar and spice.
Although she is small,
An infant yet in size,
She is going to be
Quite a unique surprise;
For once she is grown,
It won't be too very long
Before she'll make
A decision so great
That'll affect so many lives
Of a generational size.

The impact of her life
Will be as a shining light
That'll shine upon men's path
Leading them away from Divine wrath
And into the loving embrace
Of a savior's amazing grace.

As Long As You're Content

As long as you're content
To see through carnal eyes,
You'll never see
The truth of God
Through this world's disguise.
As long as you're content
To hear through carnal ears,
You'll never hear
The voice of God
Throughout all of your years.

As long as you're content
In the place that you share,
You'll never have strength enough
To defeat any lion or bear,
As did the shepherd boy
That became a king,
And drove away demons
Whenever He'd play and sing.

As long as you're content
To be just what you are,

You'll never discover
That potential shining star,
That'll brighten the path
Of many a lost soul,
That by its light
Would find the path
To be made completely whole.
So, hunger and thirst
For the truth
Of God's Living Word;
And change your heart
So that by you
Its message will be heard.
No, don't allow
Yourself to be
Content with what you see;
But be determined
To hear His voice;
And He will set you free.

Your hungry soul
Must press to see
Beyond the here and now.
Don't be content
To only know
What's beneath your brow.

You'll need to hear
That still small voice
Gently calling, "This way";
So, just listen
Ever intently
As you seek and pray.

B's

Basic Understanding

To understand the basic principles of life;
The process of growth through resistance to strife;
The necessary elements of both nutrients and water;
The need for companionship to nurture one another;
The order of a family and its reproduction;
The need for training and disciplined instruction;
This wisdom can only come by Divine revelation
From the God that Fathered this entire creation.

While wisdom's the goal of the disciplined life;
Understanding's the journey through daily strife;
For it's the struggle and strain of our mind and emotion
That helps us make sense of all life's commotion.

If we'd never stretch to life comprehend
We'd never grow nor our mind expand
Sufficient enough for us to grasp
The real meaning of life or even the need to ask
The Holy One for Divine revelation
To shine its light on all life's situations.

✫ ✫ ✫

Behold, How Subtle

Behold, how subtle
Our enemy is
To attempt his quiet
Illusive kiss
To allure the righteous
Into a path
Of compromise with
The ways of wrath,
To lure the simple
Into the snare
Of which they are
So unaware,
To lure the trusting
Into the way
Of those beguiled
And now enslaved.
Oh, how to avoid
His tempting ways,

To live a life
That God will praise,
As He did Job
Before his test.
Oh, read the Book
To hear the rest.

Better Not To Start

Not everyone can do
What it actually takes
To stop the momentum
Of sin in its tracks;
For once you're on
The pathway of sin
You're oblivious to
The way to win.
The exit signs
Just pass so fast,
You almost cannot see them
Until they're already past.
So, it's better not to start
Down the pathway of sin,
Then to find yourself into
The fire falling in.

Beyond That Door

Just what is beyond that door
That you keep closed so tight?
Is it something that makes you ashamed,
Or are you just full of fright?
Are you trying to hide
All of your sin and pride,
Or don't you want to be
Set completely free?

Behold I stand at that door
And I knock, and knock, and knock;
And you can be real sure
That I'm standing firm as a rock;
So just release those fears
And give to me your guilt.
Unlock that door

That you have built.
Invite me in
And your will see
Just what it means
To be set free.

Bible

"B" is for the BRIGHTNESS
Of its light through all of time.

"I" is for its INSTRUCTION
To help us to tow the line.

"B" is for its BOLDNESS
To tell it like it is.

"L" is for the LOVE
And grace to live like this.

"E" is for the ENLIGHTENMENT
We find within its text.
And its words are sent
To help us
To face what's coming next.

Big Mistake ›››››››››
Little Mistake

The question that faces many of us today is not whether or not we will make a mistake; for I'm sure you'll agree that the Bible teaches that we all are imperfect beings "born in sin and shapen in iniquity." Everyone of us will make mistakes. But the real question lies in the magnitude of the consequences of the actual mistakes that we will make. For example: how we are baptized. Is water baptism really going to make a difference in our eternal condition before God, or is it just another ceremony? Is immersion or sprinkling the right method? Oh, and what about the name—Father, Son, and Holy Ghost, or Jesus name? If you spent time researching water baptism in the Word of God and came to the conclusion that it is really not important at all; and didn't obey it; then die only to find out that it was the very thing that kept you out of Heaven; would that be a BIG MISTAKE or a LITTLE MISTAKE? On the other hand; if after your research you came to the conclusion that water baptism in Jesus name for the remission of sins was absolutely necessary to make it into Heaven; and you then obeyed it; only to die and find out it really wasn't important at all; for you would have still enjoyed eternal life *with Jesus Christ if you would have never been baptized at all; would that be a BIG MISTAKE or LITTLE MISTAKE? I'm sure you'll agree that the first scenario would be the BIG MISTAKE and the second one the LITTLE MISTAKE. So, on this basis, I implore you to consider prayerfully Acts 2:37-39. Weigh it out with all speed and diligence; for it possibly could be the most important time you will have ever spent in your entire life here on Earth.*

Blessings For Kindness

Many times
We ask God for things,
But we ask amiss,
And count that He
Did not provide
For our prayer or our wish.
But God does not
Fulfill our lusts,
Those desires for selfish ends.
But He does provide
For things we need
As soon as our faith begins
To comprehend
His goodness to us
Does not have self in mind,
But those around us
That we might bless
As He teaches us to be kind.

Breaking Bread

All too often,
We forget
That breaking bread
Is where it's at.
It's not in drinking
Too much wine,
Nor in the grapes
Right off the vine.
It's not in the money
We spent that night,
Nor in that
We did not fight.
It's not in how
Much time was spent,
Nor in what
We might have sent;
For God knows
About all that;
But breaking bread
Is where it's at.
It's not in that
We laughed awhile,

Nor in that
We got to smile.
It's not in words
We should have said,
Nor in those
We should have fed.
It's not in people
We should have met,
Nor in how
We did not fret;
For God knows
About all that;
But breaking bread
Is where it's at.
When He spoke words
That burned within,
And walked upon
The road with friends,
They knew not
From whence He was '
Til to break bread
Was what He must.
Revelation came
To them through that;
For breaking bread
Is where it's at.

Breaking Strongholds

Breaking strongholds
Involves surrender
To the voice or direction
Of the Almighty God;
As well as complete faith
And trust in Him
While upon this old
Earthly road you trod.

You must first
Acknowledge the fact
That your enemy has had
This specific influence in your life;
Then a concentrated effort
To take authority
Which actually can involve
Much spiritual strife.

But once this strife is over,
And victory has been found;
You will want to take some steps
To keep the enemy from coming back around.

You want to build a wall
Or a standard of defense
Established upon righteous principles,
Then keep it up as a fence
To protect your life
From the attempts of your enemy
To bind you again
And keep you bound and not free.

C's

Calvary

"C" is for the CHRIST
That died upon this hill.

"A" is for the AWESOME
Power of His will.

"L" is for the LOVE
He displayed in going there.

"V" is for the VICTORY
He won for us to share.

"A" is for the ANSWERS
We can now have through His name.

"R" is for the REDEMPTION
That His spilt blood became.

"Y" is for His YEARNING
For us to come to Him.

And all of this spells CALVARY
The altar for all sin.

Camp Meeting

Camp meeting,
The air of expectancy;
An atmosphere of excitement;
For thousands of people are coming
From literally everywhere.
Some are coming to give;
Some to receive;
Most with hearts wide open
Looking and expecting
For God Almighty
To do great things.
Some that come
Will be lonely.
Some will be hurting,
Physically, emotionally, financially.
Some are coming full of faith and victory.
Some are coming empty and distraught.
Some are saying
In their hearts,
"Maybe, just maybe,
This will be the time
That God will meet me

In my need".
And, sad to say,
Sometimes they leave disillusioned;
But, you see,
That really doesn't have to be.
They could leave completely set free.
What do you think it is
That keeps them bound?
Could it be you?
Or, could it be me?

Can I Really Do All Things?

I can do all things
through Christ
which strengtheneth me.
Php 4:13

When you consider this word,
"I can do all things"
From a disabled point of view,
Makes it hard
To grasp the faith
That all things
You can do.
Until you consider
This one fact
And count it fully true,
That Christ is not
Disabled here.
The disability lies
In you.
And when you trust

Fully in Him
You'll find that this is true.
That you can actually
Do all things.
In Him all things
You can do.

Can We Cast On God All Our Cares?

Can we cast on God
All our cares
Fully confident
That He is there?
The answer to
This question lies
In the fact
That Satan lies
And questions each
And every word
That you and I
Have ever heard
Of what our God
Has promised us.
Why else would
He Make such a fuss?

Whatever Satan says
Is not so,
You can just believe
The opposite though.

★ ★ ★

Cast It All

When the battle's raging
Deep within your soul;
And you feel all divided;
And desire to be made whole;
When you can't bear the burden
Of your problems any more;
Cast it all at the feet
Of the lowly Savior.
When your life becomes a heavy
Burden on your mind;
And peace seems to be
Just too hard for you to find;
And the pressures of this life
Upon your soul seems to pour;
Cast it all at the feet
Of the lowly savior.
For though the cares of life
Seems so much bigger than you are;
And you feel like an ant
Fighting in a world of war;
Remember God is bigger
Than any foe you'll ever fight;

And will be fighting for you
As you stand for what is right.
There is no problem big enough
That can stop His mighty hand;
And He'll be working for you
As you commit unto His plan;
So don't ever stop your fighting
'Til you're through victory's door,
But cast all your heavy burdens
At the feet of the Savior.

Casting My Care

To cast my care
Upon the Lord
Would mean I don't
Any of them hoard;
For to hold them close
To my dear heart
Would in itself
Not to be smart;
For burdens born
And carried long
Wear out the soul
Making it forlorn;
But casting them down
At Jesus feet
Can bring my soul
Much rest and peace.

☆ ☆ ☆

Cathy

"C" is for the CARE
You manifest in prayer.

"A" is for the ANGELS
That attend when you are there.

"T" is for the TIME
That you spent down on your knees.

"H" is for the HOLINESS
Of God for He is so pleased.

"Y" is for the YEARNING
Of your soul whenever you pray.

And I wrote this poem for you;
After hearing you pray today.

Celebrating Christmas

Is Christmas for the present;
Or is Christmas for the past;
Or what about the future;
How long should Christmas last?
Is Christmas 'til tomorrow;
Or the day after that?
Should I wait for Christmas future;
Or should I search for Christmas past?
Should I celebrate it now;
Or celebrate it then;
And if neither one of these;
Then please tell me when?
To celebrate Christ's birth;
No one really knows the date;
For December twenty-fifth
Is really a mistake.

The answer to these questions
Are not really hard to find;
For Christ's birth should be celebrated
Most all of the time.

Chains

There are chains that hold.
There are chains that bind
That keep a man
From the crimson tide,
Held so strong,
And kept in place
By the pride of heart
That resists God's grace.

There are chains that bind.
There are chains that hold
That keep the heart
So hot, not cold,
Held so strong,
And kept in place
By the humble spirit
Committed through grace.

The chains that hold,
And the chains that bind
Your life are one
Of these two kinds.

One or the other
Are kept in place
By choices made
Through the gift of grace.

★ ★ ★

Children Let's Count

One and one is two.
Two and one is three.
You know that Jesus Christ
Came to set us free.
Three and one is four.
Four and one is five.
God is not dead.
He is very much alive.
Five and one is six.
Six and one is seven.
You know He's coming back
To take us all to Heaven.
Seven and one is eight.
Eight and one is nine.
Put your trust in Jesus;
And you will sure be fine.

Nine and one is ten.
So, let's put on a grin;
For that you and I
Are gonna count it once again.

Choose Your Prison Wisely

Choose your prison wisely,
Oh man of Planet Earth;
For you'll come to know
You're bound for one
From the moment of your birth.
Some men are bound
To spend their days
Bound up and bridled
By sinful ways;
While others choose
To walk by faith
Bound to a promise
Of a better place.
To be a prisoner,
We all will be,
Some of sin and degradation,
Others of righteous liberty.

So make your choice,
And make it fast;
For soon all opportunity
Will completely pass;
But choose wisely
And you will see
That your choice will determine
Your eternal destiny.

Christmas

"C" is for the CHRIST CHILD
That was born upon this day.

"H" is for the HOLINESS
Of God upon display.

"R" is for the RIGHTEOUSNESS
That was shining all around.

"I" is for the INCREDIBLE THING
That happened in this town.

"S" is for the SUFFERING
That He had to go through.

"T" is for the TRUTH He brought
To deliver me and you.

"M" is for the MIRACULOUS
Way that Jesus came.

"A" is for the ANGELS
Who revealed to us His name.

"S" is for the SALVATION
We now have through faith in Him.
And all of this spell CHRISTMAS,
The day it all began.

Cleared For Take Off

"So, you want to be
Cleared for take off;
Do you?
Well, you haven't even
Filed an acceptable
Flight plan yet.
And,
As 'Air Traffic Controller',
It is my responsibility
To watch the air
In order to help you
To avoid collisions,
Storms,
Mountains,
And anything else
That might keep you
From reaching
Your destination;
But, my friend,
Unless you file
An acceptable flight plan,
I just cannot

Clear you
"For take off".

Now, as Christians,
Jesus Christ is
Our "Air Traffic Controller".
Throughout our life,
He helps us
To avoid the collisions,
The storms,
And the mountains that get in our way;
But should we have a collision,
He is there
To pick up the pieces;
And should we fly into a storm,
He is there
To guide us safely through it;
And should a mountain be in our way;
He is there
To lift us above it.
And,
In our worse case scenario,
Should we crash,
Jesus is there
To help us sort through
The wreckage of our life
In order to help us start
All over again.
Oh yes,

And if we want to be
"Cleared for take off"
On that great
And glorious day of Christ's return,
We have to file
An acceptable flight plan
With the great
"Air Traffic Controller"
Of the Eternal realm,
Jesus Christ.

Come And Dine

Jesus is always
Inviting somebody
To supper.
He never tires
Of having any
Invited guests.
And so,
As His ambassadors,
His desire for us
Is that
We should participate
In the process
Of the invitation,
So we may also
Participate in His joy,
As we rejoice with Him
In the response
Of those who come.
But we must also
Be prepared to mourn with Him
Over those who refuse to come.
Oh, but this mourning

To us will be a blessing;
For though it "may endure for a night,
Joy will come in the morning".
And though we may grieve
Over some lost soul
That we invited to the party,
That refused to come,
God has still promised us
"Joy" in the midst of "sorrow",
"Beauty" in the place of "ashes",
"A garment of praise"
In the place of
"A spirit of heaviness".
And His "promises" to us
Are "not slack".
He fulfills every "jot and tittle",
Crosses every "t",
And dots every "I";
For "the promises of God
Are Yea and Amen
To them that believe".

So, we must busy ourselves
By inviting everyone we see
To His Great Supper,
To the Grandest Dinner Party of all time;
For truly "the Master calleth,
Come and Dine".

Come, My Beloved

Come, My beloved
Into the sanctuary
Of My presence.
Come on in
And you will find
That I will be
A haven of rest;
For when you're tired
Of worldly cares
You can believe
That I will be there
To help you with
Your heavy load,
And give you grace
To walk this road.

Come, My beloved
And praise My name,
And I will help you
Bear the strain;
And as you lift
Up Holy hands,

While you surrender
All of your plans,
I can work out
The rest of your life,
And give you strength
To bear your strife.

Committed

To be committed
Is to think of first,
When life's at its best,
And when life's at its worst.
It is to carry out
And to fulfill,
To stand beside
Even until,
To want the best for,
And to be concerned
When some entrapment
Has not yet been learned,
To be ready to encourage
When the down is felt,
And to forgive,
And eliminate guilt.

To be committed
Is what we ought to be,
First us to God,
Then me to you,
And you to me.

Confirmation

Lord, I need a confirmation
Of this path you're leading me down;
For your word says to be careful,
And to consider where you're bound.
Before taking the steps to do
Those things you're asking of me,
Confirmation can only
Strengthen my faith
And help me to believe.
Lord, please send me confirmation.
Make solid places for my feet;
So that when I do step out,
I will not end up in defeat.
Confirmation can only bring
To me the victory,
Help me understand Your will;

And from worry set me free;
Give me a solid place
That I can stand;
So that I can then be used
To reach some other lost man.

Considerate Christmas Celebration

Christmas is the season
Of merriment and cheer
For most that get involved
In blessing others every year;
But for some that are alone
Without a friend in whom to confide,
This time of year consumes
Much of their inner pride;
For they tend to believe
That no one really cares
Enough to include them
And their Christmas share.
So, consider the lonely soul
As you celebrate this time.
Consider that they're hurting
For a friend, or two, or nine.

Invite that lonely soul to Christmas;
And include them in your plans.
You just might make their day,
And they forever be your friend.

Contending With Horses?

Jeremiah 12:5 "If thou hast run with the footmen, and they
have wearied thee, then how canst thou contend with horses?
And in the land of peace, wherein thou trustedst, they wearied
thee, then how wilt thou do in the swelling of the Jordan?"

When I have grown weary
With just keeping up,
The footmen all marching
Completely wound up,
How can I even begin
With horses to contend?
Although there's no way
My two feet could run as fast as four,
I won't at all give up
So as not to continue anymore;
For I think the best way to deal
With this incoming tide
Is to get upon my horse of worship
And just ride, ride, ride.
You see, my strength is not my own
When I'm worshiping my King.
It's His joy that I ride

106

When I His praises sing.
So when I have to deal
With this incoming tide,
I'll just get upon my horse of worship
And just ride, ride, ride.

Counted Worthy

Feeling so unworthy
Of the blessings that God sends
Makes it so very hard
Unto His will to bend;
For when the blessings come,
We quickly watch them go;
When we really should have invested,
Then to watch them grow.

When we think of life,
And how we all have sinned;
Not one of us are worthy;
Not one of us should win;
But because of Jesus Christ,
And the work of Calvary,
We can be counted worthy
And set completely free.

Covenant

"C" is for the COMMITMENT
That true COVENANT requires.

"O" is for the OBEDIENCE
That true COVENANT inspires.

"V" is for the VICTORY
That total commitment can bring.

"E" is for the ENCOURAGEMENT of having
Someone to which you can cling.

"N" is for the NEARNESS you feel
Whenever you do commit.

"A" is for the ASSURANCE of
The vows with which you are knit.

"N" is for Never *forgetting*
These vows that you have made.

"T" is for being always True*;*
Never giving anything in trade.

★ ★ ★

Crossing The Line

Crossing the line
From right to wrong
Will open the door
For one who's strong
To enter in and destroy
The righteous life
Of the real McCoy.

Crossing the line
From wrong to right
Will open the door
For the light
Of the Holy One
To enter in
And to drive out
The ways of sin.

Crossroads

I'm standing
At these crossroads
In the valley
Of decision
Trying to determine
Which way to go
And the extent
Of my revision.
I must review
All the facts
In order to make
The wisest choice;
So that when
I do look back,
I'll have reason
To rejoice.
I dare not tarry
Too long right here;
For more travelers
Must pass by here.
If I wait too very long
To make up my mind

I may not be able
The right way to find;
And some other traveler
In time may not see
The path that will lead them
To victory.

D's

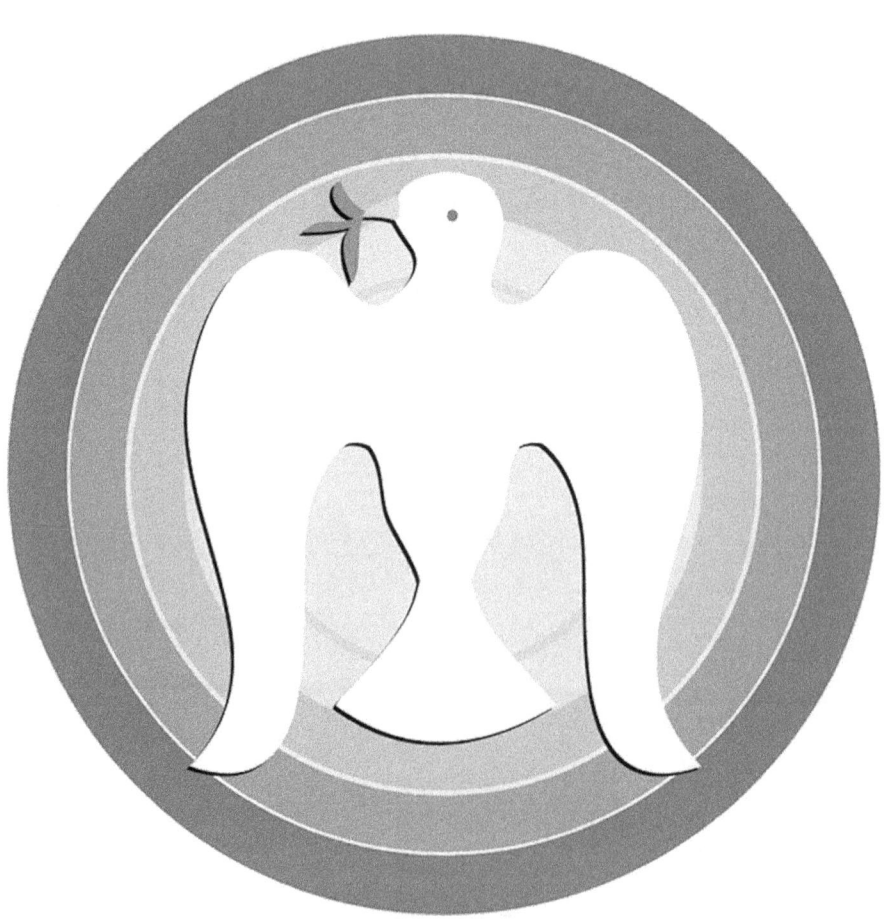

Dating

Dating is for real,
Not for a game;
For keeps,
Not for fame;
For love,
Not for shame;
For peace,
Not for pain.
So, when you date,
Don't play around.
Sure,
Have some fun;
But consider where you're bound.
There are some things
That, doing them,
You don't want to be found.
There are some people that
You need not be around.

You see,
Dating
Is not a game.
It is for real.
And it is your emotions
That you play around with;
And it is your pain that
You will feel.

Dear Adam: From God

How much do you love Me?
Can I count the ways?
Do you love Me enough
To give Me all the praise?
Do you love Me enough
To open up your heart;
And let Me fill it
To the full, not just in part?
Do you love Me enough
To consecrate your life;
Making the sacrifices
That can end all your strife?
How much do you love Me?
Will you walk with Me today;
Or will you even bow your knee
For a moment; just to pray?
Do you love Me enough
To take Me by the hand;
And let Me guide you through
This dark and dreary land?
Do you love Me enough
To open up My book?

I want to show you things.
Oh please, take a look.
How much do you love Me?
Please let Me show you man;
My Divine purpose;
My Divine plan.
How much do you love Me?
Can I really count the ways,
The ways that you love Me,
And give Me all the praise?

Dear God:

I know I don't deserve
The kindness you have shown
All of these years.
Oh, my, haven't they flown?
Please forgive me for
All of the wasted time,
When I should have focused
Upon what was Thine.
Help me now to see
How to be so wise
As to redeem the time.
Oh, please, open my eyes
To see the quickest way
To win souls to thee;
For Lord I'm looking
For more than two or three.
Jesus, I'm asking this very moment
For you to use my life
To help many people
Find eternal life.
Direct my steps, oh Lord,
As I walk each day.

119

Help me to be more sensitive
Is what I really pray.
I ask this all above
In Jesus precious name.
Lord, it is Your will that I want to claim.

Definition Of A Bad Day

How do I define
A bad day?
Well, it's one where I
Forgot to pray;
Forgot to take
A solemn look
For instruction from
God's Holy book;
Forgot to listen
For His voice;
Forgot to make
That better choice;
Forgot to ask
For answers needed;
Forgot to let
My cause be pleaded;
Forgot to seek
His presence out;
Forgot to close
The door on doubt;
Forgot to knock
On Heaven's door;

Forgot to ask
My God for more.
Oh, how do I define
A bad day?
Well, my friend,
It's one where I forgot to pray.

Delivered

Enticed by her
Seductive ways,
He became
Truly amazed;
For all that he
Had once stood for
Was suddenly engaged
In an internal war.
Drawn away by
His heart's desire,
Set aflame by
Sensual fire,
He then began
To meditate
Upon how he was
To claim his stake.
Unwilling to hear
The warnings of
Godly men and
The words of love,
He took some steps,
Set out a plan,

How to pursue
This woman;
But before that he
Could then pursue
All that he
Was planning to do,
He saw a figure
Of a Cross,
And then began
To count the cost.
Then with the sound
Of conviction's words,
He cried repentant tears
That his God heard;
And within a moment
Or two in time,
He was delivered
Then to shine.

Desire

Desire can be your enemy,
Or desire can be your friend.
It really just all depends
Upon that desire's end.
If desire leads you down
The road to destruction;
Then to follow its path
Can be to your demise;
But if it leads you to peace
Through disciplined instruction;
Then the agony of training
Is merely just a disguise.

✫ ✫ ✫

Disappointment

Disappointment
Is the product of
The expectation
Of human love;
For when you expect
Your love returned,
And then find out
That it was spurned;
Oh what pain
You start to feel,
Because your hopes
Had seemed so real;
But when just beyond
Your reach are they
Is when you really

Need to pray
For comfort from
The Holy One
That can heal
Your heart
So broken.

Disciple

Sometimes I've heard
That still small voice,
That gentle tug
To make Him my choice.

Sometimes I've felt
The sting of the hand,
The firm words
Of a sharp reprimand.

Sometimes I've heard
An audible voice
Calling with authority
To make His way my choice.

Sometimes I've felt
A slap in the face,
A shout in my ear
To quicken my pace.

Sometimes I've been
Cut off from all men
With only a desire
To be alone with Him.

Distant Light

Watching from a distance
This Man from Galilee
Can hardly set you, my friend,
As a poor old sinner free.
Although just having Him
Barely in your sight
Really does mean
That you have got
Just a little Light;
But unless you seek to follow
Just where this Light does lead,
You'll find yourself,
Once again,
Doing those dark deeds.
Now, should you decide to walk
Down this dimly lit path
That His Light has exposed;
You'll soon discover
Just how much brighter
His Light will begin to glow,
Until your whole life
Is illuminated by

And filled with such glorious Light
That all those that are around you
Can see through you
To His Glory that's
Reflecting into their night.

Divine Inspiration

Under the inspiration
Of the Holy Ghost
The Psalmist wrote a song
Which about God did boast.
And as he continued writing
Day in and day out,
He built up our faith,
Quenching much of our doubt.
This inspiration that flowed
Through this Psalmist's pen
Still flows today
Helping us to win.
Each and every time
We read what this Psalmist wrote,
And receive its message,
It gives us faith and hope.

So, let this inspiration
That flowed through David's pen
Lift you up in spirit
So that you might win.

Divine Intervention

Walking the line
On the edge of life
Can fill one's heart
So full of strife
That one cannot tell
Just where he actually stands
And is preparing for
The sharp reprimand.
The question that lies
Within the heart of a man
Is weather or not
He can actually stand
Against the winds
And the waves of desire
That wants to set
His soul on fire.
This fire would then burn
Down deep within;
And stain the soul
With the mark of sin.
Unless the Grace
Of Almighty God

Will intervene,
This road we'll trod.
Because God is not willing
That anyone should die
With the stain of sin
Blinding the eye,
He has sent us His mercy
To our life intervene,
So that His blood
Can make our soul clean.

Divine Strategy

There was a strategy
Used by Jesus Christ
That bought for us victory
Over sin and strife.
Now this strategy
Has not been used by most,
Although it is how
One receives the Holy Ghost.
This was the strategy
That preceded the Cross
Which insured that Jesus Christ
Would not suffer loss.
What was this strategy
Used by Christ our Lord?
It was that of surrender
To the prophetic Word.

When He said, "Not my will,
But Thine be done;"
It insured that our victory
Would then very soon be won.

Don't Stay Out There

When reading the Word
Becomes just a chore;
And praying to God
Is not much more;
When you don't feel His presence
Coming at all to you;
Then let me ask you, Brother,
What are you gonna do?

When you can't find the way
Through this old world;
And when you try to pray
You can't seem to find the words;
And things are built up
Way down deep inside;
And you just can't overcome
Your very own pride;

Will you stay out there
So very all alone;
Or will your reach out
To anyone

To help you seek God
And renew
Your relationship
With this God that's true?

Dress For The Occasion

Before you go out for the day
Dress for the occasion
Knowing this one thing
That living for God
Is like fighting a war.
Only the battle ground
Is within the hearts
And minds of men.
The weapons to fight with
Aren't guns, knives, or spears,
But are prayer, the word, praise,
And worship in the Spirit.
And unless you are prepared,
You will get knocked down
Or wounded.
So, dress for the occasion by
Putting on the whole armor of God.

*"Wherefore take unto you the whole armor of God,
that you may be able to withstand in the evil day,
and having done all, to stand.
Ephesians 6:13*

Drive And Pray

When the storm is raging,
And its pouring all around;
And you don't want to chance
Getting on the road to town;
But you need something desperately,
And have to anyway;
You get out in the weather,
And just drive and pray.

When you hit a patch of water
Which makes you hydroplane,
You then begin to panic
For steering is insane;
You call on the name of Jesus
And control is then restored,
It makes you very thankful
You've come to know the Lord.

E's

Easter

"*E*" *is for* EVERYONE
That's the reason that he came.

"*A*" *is for the* AUTHORITY HE GIVES
Over sin and shame.

"*S*" *is for the* SALVATION *we have*
Through faith in HIS NAME.

"*T*" *is for the* TRUTH *that sets us free*
Again and again.

"*E*" *is for the* ENCOURAGEMENT *we get*
From spending time alone with HIM.

"*R*" *is for the* REST HE GIVES
As we learn to trust in HIS NAME.

His EXAMPLE
Showed us HOW TO COPE.
His ASSURANCE
Gave our hearts NEW HOPE.
His SURRENDER
Brought us VICTORY.

His Touch
Gave us Liberty.

His Everlasting Arms
Gave us real Support.
His Redeeming Blood
Gave us A Brand New Start.

Elevate Me, Oh Lord

Elevate my thoughts, oh Lord,
That I may catch a glimpse of yours.
Elevate my ways, oh Lord,
That I may walk on Heavenly shores.
Elevate my love
That I may love the unlovable.
Elevate my sensitivity
That I may touch the untouchable.
Elevate my knowledge
That I may,
Above all,
Know You.
Elevate my vision, oh Lord,
That I may see the invisible.

Elevate my faith
That I may taste
The ultimate victory.
Elevate my wisdom
That I may be wise enough
To obey Thee.

Eternal Regrets

Where did the time go;
The years that I spent
Running to and fro?
Why couldn't I just stop
And take one serious look
At what was written in
God's Holy book?

Man, time sure did fly
While I was having my fun;
But now I only have
Enough time to just
Flat out run;
For if I'm going to do
All that God's will is
I can't even take
A little bit of time
For any of this other biz.

Time is so very, very short
Before Jesus Christ returns.
I really do have to
The midnight oil burn;
For that which God
Has called me to do
Will require all of me now;
And that really is the truth.

F's

Faith, Hope, And Love

Faith, hope and love
Are truly gifts from above.
Faith comes by hearing
From God's Holy word.
And hope comes from trusting
In what you have heard.
Love comes through giving
Oneself to the Lord.
And all this together
Will bless you all the more.

✫ ✫ ✫

Faithful Men

Watching with
An unfaithful eye,
She planned and plotted
Just how to try
To gain the attention
Of this faithful man
To cause him to fall
From his faithful stand.
Now if she succeeds
She might rejoice
For a time or season
Cause of her choice;
But little known
Is what she'll face
In the hereafter
Beyond this life course race.
Faithful men
Don't live for now;
But continually focus
Upon just how
To make it through
To this life's end

Without committing
The moral sin.
The reward of such
A righteous life
Cannot be compared
To this earthly plight.

★ ★ ★

Family Weekend

Family weekend,
A time to gather
For fellowship and fun
Where all the children
Can come together
To play and run.
Families camping out
Underneath the stars,
Pitching tents
In a time of celebration
Of what community has meant.
It's a time of bonding
For both church and family
To strengthen the cords of love
That truly set us free.
It's a time to focus on
The inner qualities of
Those brothers and sisters
That are bound to us in love.

Fasting

"F" is for the FLESH
That you are trying to overcome.

"A" is for the ANSWERS,
For you hope to get some.

"S" is for this SACRIFICE
That you've chosen to give.

"T" is for the TRUTH
That you have chosen to live.

"I" is for the INSTRUCTION
You desire to get through prayer.

"N" is for the "No's"
You tell yourself when you're there.

*"G" is for the G*RACE
Of God that waits for you.

*And F*ASTING *is one thing*
That will help you make it through.

Fear

Some say that
Fear is healthy.
Some say that
Fear is not.
Some say that
Fear has torment;
And is divisive
In its plot.
Some say
In fear is safety.
Some say that
Fear brings pain.
Some say that
Fear's the reason
They call on
Jesus name.

Feed The Hungry

Feed the hungry.
Clothe the poor;
And God will bless
You all the more.

Help the needy
In word and deed;
And reap God's blessings
From that seed.

Live your life
To give away
Your abundance;
And you will say

That you've been given
More than your share
Due to a heart
That's filled with care.

Fellowship

"F" is for the FEELING
Of acceptance that you feel.
"E" is for the ENLIGHTENMENT
That sharing His word can reveal.
"L" is for the LIVES
Of those who really care.
"L" is for the LOVE
That we so often share.
"O" is for the ONENESS
We feel with everyone.
"W" is for the WILLINGNESS
Of all those that have come.
"S" is for how SPECIAL
Everyone is to you.
"H" is for the HAPPINESS
That this can bring to you.

"I" is for your INVOLVEMENT
In everybody's lives.
"P" is for the PURPOSE OF GOD
For together we will survive.

Fifth Sunday Dinner

Chopped beef steak,
All nice and juicy;
Mashed potatoes and gravy,
Made by Aunt Lucy;
Buttered corn and bread,
Piping hot to the touch;
And chocolate cream pie,
Just a little too much;
All this and much more
Is what could be found
At the First Pentecostal Church
Fifth Sunday
Dinner on the Ground.

Fried chicken in baskets,
A whole table full;
Catsup and fried taters;
Corn on the cob in the hull;
Black-eyed peas, butter beans,
And more of that such;
Fresh baked strawberry pie,
Now ain't that too much;

All this and much more
Is what could be found
At the First Pentecostal Church
Fifth Sunday
Dinner on the Ground.

Pastors and their wives;
Youth groups and choirs;
Evangelists would drive
For all sorts of hours;
Singing groups would come
With their bands all in stride,
Just to come and sing,
And share their talents with pride;
All this and much more
Is what could be found
At the First Pentecostal Church
Fifth Sunday
Dinner on the Ground.

Elders and Deacons;
Laymen of all sorts;
Board Members and Trustees,
All playing their parts;
Missionaries on furlough
Raising money for trips;
Politicians with their aids;
And so many more V.I.P.'s;
All this and much more

Is what could be found
At the First Pentecostal Church
Fifth Sunday
Dinner on the Ground.

★ ★ ★

Fight For The Right

I was looking for the light,
When I entered a fight,
Where everyone seemed in the right;
But only one was.

Although it was dark,
I caught a glimpse of a spark
With the victorious remark,
"In the name of Jesus."

By the end of the fight,
The room was filled with the light
Of the one who was true and right,
The Lord Jesus.

Flowers

Flowers bloom,
And flowers fade,
Only for life to make a trade;
For as seasons come,
And seasons go,
Flowers seed;
And those seeds grow;
Now, when they're grown,
New flowers bloom,
Only to fade,
And then make room
For the next seasons flowers
To come and go,
Or for some other plant
To spring up and grow.

☆ ☆ ☆

"F" is for your FAITHFULNESS
That keeps you standing strong.

"O" is for your OBEDIENCE
That keeps you out of the wrong.

"C" is for your CONCENTRATION
That helps you zero in.

"U" is for your UNDERSTANDING
That will help you win.

"S" is for your STEWARDSHIP
That makes you worthy of trust.

And all of these will help you FOCUS
On the things that you must.

Forgiveness

Forgiveness comes to those who forsake
The path they've traveled on
To find a path much higher than
The one they have been on.
Forgiveness runs away from those
Who stubbornly refuse
To get off the path they've traveled on
Which path they still choose.

Forgiveness comes to those who seek
For a way to change their life
By calling upon Jesus Christ
To help them through all their strife.
Forgiveness runs away from those
That seek a selfish end
That only want to appear to seek
The right path before their friends.

Forgiveness comes to those that are
Truly sorry for their sin
Not sorry that they have been caught
Sinning once again.

Forgiveness runs away from those
That only regret they're caught
And will not turn their heart to God
To seek just what they ought.

Forgiveness comes to those who pray
Unto God with honest hearts
Ready to turn from all their ways
From sin to then depart.

Four Cedar Walls

Four cedar walls,
In this attic so high,
Oh, so alone,
So alone am I;
Locked up in this closet
So that maybe I
Can pray past my fears.
At least I can try.

Four cedar walls,
If they could testify;
They'd tell you of how
Very hard I did try.
They'd tell of all
The tears I did cry;
Locked up in this attic,
In this attic so high.

Four cedar walls,
One window, one door;
Day after day,
I'd seek Him some more;

So afraid of what
I was seeking for;
Yet earnestly seeking
Locked behind this great door.

One week went by;
Then went by two.
If I do not find Him;
Oh, what should I do?
Stay locked up behind
All fearful and blue
These four cedar walls;
Just what should I do?

Four cedar walls,
I can't stay right here;
Locked up behind
These four walls of fear.
I've got to step out;
Step out now by faith;
If I'm ever going to find
Some more of God's grace.

Though I'm not real sure
Which way I should go;
If I stay right here,
I know I won't grow.
So, I'm stepping out.
I'm telling fear, "No;

You can't hold me here;
I'm going to go."

So, by facing those fears;
I now have gained faith;
And found that my God
Has given more grace;
And all that I've needed
To run this great race.
Now, I'm determined
To just keep in pace.

Francis

The "F" is for her FAITH
That she expresses from day to day.

The "R" is for her RESPONSE
To the Almighty when she prays.

The "A" is for the ANGELS
That attend when she's in prayer.

The "N" is for that NEVER
Will she loose for she will remain there.

The "C" is for the CARE
She expresses to those in need.

The "I" is for the INCREDIBLE POWER
She finds as God's Word she heeds.

The "S" is for her SACRIFICE
That she renders unto the Lord.

And her name is FRANCIS,
Whom God will bless with a tremendous reward.

G's

Gift Or Investment?

When a sacrifice
Ceases to be voluntary,
It also ceases
To be acceptable;
For where
There is no willingness
Left to give,
What is given
Ceases to be a gift;
And becomes
A purchase price;
Because once it is given,
A return
Is then expected
On the investment.

When a true gift is given,
No return is actually expected;
Because what is given
Is not viewed
As an investment;
But a gift.

Glasses

We all wear glasses
Of many different sorts.
Some are made of plastic.
Some are made of hearts.
The lenses may be glass
Designed to magnify,
Or possibly made of words
To merely amplify
Many areas of our lives
That we may need to see,
And may even define to us
What it means to be free.
You see,
Glasses are for sight
To help you focus upon
The path that is before you
Whether it's right
Or whether it is wrong;

So that you may decide
Whether to continue on,
Or to stop and turn around
Based upon what you see
Through these glasses
You have found.

God Bless You

May the Grace of God be with you
In all you try to do.
May God's Spirit be ever present
And may your heart be ever true.
May His blessings over take you
In an awesome way.
May you always remember
To seek the Lord and pray.
May you never think too highly,
Taking pride within yourself;
So you may always then exalt Him;
And find spiritual wealth.
May the Love of God find a place
Deep within your heart;
And fill you with compassion;
While meet other's needs you start.

May you live in great expectancy
Of the things that God will do.
May your faith be ever growing,
And God's presence ever new.

God Blessed America

God blessed America;
And what did America do?
For many, many years
She flourished and she grew;
Because she helped the Alien
And welcomed them at her door;
Then God blessed America;
And blessed her all the more.
So she continued to flourish;
'Til by war this world was tore;
Then she stepped into the picture
For to help liberty's cause;
And God still blessed America.
No, His blessings did not pause.
God continued on His blessings
Through a second world of war
Where America again stepped in
When again by war this world was torn.

Now at a new horizon
In time she marches on.
Her attitude is changing

181

And causing God to mourn;
For what America is now doing
With the blessings He has sent
Is squandering it all on selfishness;
Upon selfish goals are they spent.

God, Why?

God, why has my life
Just twisted and turned,
Changing directions
With each lesson I've learned?
Why has prosperity?
Just flown as a plane
Each time I had set
New goals for my gain?
Just why has this life
Treated me thus?
Could it be that I'm destined
To be a big "Bust"?
Or, could it be that
I'm just Missing the mark,
And aiming this arrow
Out into the dark?

Growing In Grace

Growing in grace
Sometimes means
Enduring the trials
And tests of life.
And betimes
It just may mean
Going through seasons
Of great strife.
But as you learn
To trust the Lord
Through all the above
Growing in grace
Can reveal to you
How boundless is
God's great love.

H's

Harmony

What Does It Really Take
To live in harmony?
Tolerate the faults
And failures of so many;
Decide that you won't always
Get your own way;
Maybe even have to change
Your usual place to pray.
You may have to occasionally
Obey a different voice;
Or just have to go along
With another's choice.
You may just have to give up
Some of your personal space;
Even sometimes surrender
Your comfortable sleeping place;

Perhaps play a game or two
That you really dislike;
And give in here and there
Just to avoid a fight.

Hate

Hate,
My friend,
Is a big mistake
It'll turn you into
A real fake.
Your dignity from you
It will take.
Anything you do
Will be second rate.
Change your mind
Before it's too late.
You'll find,
My friend,
That a lot is at stake.
Another choice
You can now make.
Do it now,
For Heaven's sake.
Do not delay;
Oh, please don't wait.
You see,
My friend,

We all have a date.
If you ever want to see
Those Pearly Gates;
And absolutely avoid
That fiery lake;
The wrath of God
You can escape.
Oh yes, My friend,
Please don't hate.

Have You Heard

Have you heard
The voice of God
Speaking unto you?
Have you heard
His Holy word
As it has broken through
All the barriers
And defenses
That you have raised so high?
Have you heard
The voice of God,
And heard His heart's cry?

Have you heard His word?
Have you heard His voice?
Have you made Jesus Christ
Your ultimate choice?

Have you felt Him tugging gently
Upon your hearts strings?
Have you then decided to follow,
His praises then to sing?

He Is Truly The Light

The hustle and bustle
Of this special season
Is all due to
One special reason.
It all goes back
To one Holy night
When Mary gave birth
To the One who is Light.
As she was in labor
Laying in the hay,
Some shepherds saw angels
And fearfully prayed.
The angels did charge them
That they should fear not,
But to look for Messiah;
This message they got,
"In the city of David,
Bethlehem, by name,
The Christ child is born
In a stable," though strange.
"You'll find Him therein
Wrapped in swaddling clothes

Lying in an old manger;
So, get up and go!"
They traveled a bit,
Until they did find
What the angels had told them
About in the night.
Some two thousand years
Has past since that time;
And this child has proven
That He is truly the Light.
The hustle and bustle
Of this special season
Is all due to
One special reason.
It all goes back
To one Holy night
When Mary gave birth
To the One who is Light.
After this birth
From a journey so long
Came wise men from the east
To honor His throne.
They stopped at Herod's Palace
Thinking their journey was through;
But discovered there was more
That they had to do.
Once back on the road
The Holy star did appear

To show them to Bethlehem
Where the Christ they'd revere.
Some two thousand years has past
Since that Holy night;
And this child has proven
That He is truly the Light.

Heaven

"H" is because this is a HOLY PLACE;
For anywhere God dwells is Holy.

"E" is because this place is ETERNAL;
For it is not confined to the realm of time.

"A" is because of the ANGELS
That minister there to His Majesty.

"V" is because of the VICTORIOUS CELEBRATION there
Through Christ will be yours and mine.

"E" is because that ENTHRONED there
Will be Jesus, the Lord of all Eternity.

"N" is because that NO ONE goes there
Who did not let his light so shine.

195

Hidden Chains Of Liberty

When I look
Inside of me,
And see the chains
Of liberty,
Which keep me from
Things I would do,
So I am set free
To worship You,
I sometimes want
To reach beyond,
Break these chains,
Destroy these bonds;
But then decide
To stay behind,
So thankful for
My God so kind.
If you can't see
These hidden chains,
That bind, yet loose,
But save much pain,
They're hidden in
Commitments made,

The written word,
And spoken pledge.
Yes, this is what
Makes up the hedge
That keeps you inside,
Not on the edge.

Hidden In The Corner Of My Mind

Hidden in the corner
Of my mind
Is something that'll never
Help me unwind.
It's what makes peace
So hard for me to find;
And old man, Worry,
To become a friend of mine.
Trouble is not
Of just one kind.

When I think
From time to time
About what's hidden
In the corner of my mind.

Oh if I could only find
The answer that would
Bring me peace of mind;
Then just maybe
I could unwind;
And finally know what's hidden
In the corner of my mind.

Holiness

You're not necessarily Holy
Whenever you dress the part;
For Holiness can only be obtained
Through surrender from the heart.
It's only through submission

To God's unfolding plan
Can one obtain a Holiness
That transcends the flesh of man.
It's when your flesh does not distract
From the Christ that lives in you,
Is when your Holy relationship
With Christ can then shine through.

Holiness is not about standards;
But standards are about Holiness.
Holiness is not about dress codes;
But dress codes are about Holiness.
Holiness is not about chaste conversation;
But chaste conversation is about Holiness.
Holiness is not about the company you keep;
But the company you keep is about Holiness.

Holiness is not about stewardship;
But stewardship is about Holiness.
Holiness is not about hair length;
But hair length is about Holiness.

Holiness is not about maintaining
The distinction between male and female;
But maintaining the distinction between male and female
Is about Holiness.

Holy Ghost

"H" is for that HALLOWED
Be His Holy name.
"O" is for His ONENESS;
For He's always the same.
"L" is for His LOVE
He manifested through the Son.
"Y" is for His YEARNING
For us to Him come.

"G" is for the GIFT
That His Spirit really is.
"H" is for HIS HELP;
So we can live like this.
"O" is for His OMNIPOTENCE
That created this whole wide world.

"S" is for His SALVATION
That His great love unfurled.
"T" is for His TRUTH
That continually sets us free.

This all spells HOLY GHOST
That He'll give to you and me.

Honest

The HUMBLE MAN can learn
Wisdom from above.

The OBEDIENT MAN can learn
How to truly love.

The NEW MAN can learn
New ways to know the Lord.

The ENDURING MAN can learn
The rivers he can forge.

The SURE MAN can learn
Just how much he can stand.

The TRUE MAN can learn
What it means to be a man.

How Do I Magnify God?

Considering that God
Is, oh, so very big
That He encompasses
Each and every universe.
In fact,
If you were to lay
Galaxy after galaxy,
Galaxy after galaxy,
Until you've exhausted them all,
You still would not have reached
The end of God,
Nor even found His beginning.
So, tell me how
Do I magnify this God?
I guess I can only
Magnify
My view if Him.

★ ★ ★

How Many

How many paths
Must I travel o'er
Before I can find
Eternity's shore?

And how many places
Must I now see
Before there is found
A place for me?

And how many years
Must I now live
Before I can find
Enough grace to give?

And how many loves
Must I now possess
Before I can finally
Pass love's test?

And how much knowledge
Must I now gain
Before God's wisdom
On my soul rains.

Humble

The HONEST MAN can be
Safe from reprimand.

The UNDERSTANDING MAN can be
A safe and secure friend.

The MATURE MAN can be
A shelter from the storm.

The BRILLIANT MAN can be
A light shining in the mourn.

The LOVING MAN can be
A comfort to those in pain.

The ENCOURAGING MAN can be
One to lift them up again.

I Asked; He Said:

I asked God for Holy Fire.
He said to bring a sacrifice.
I asked God for friends unending.
He said to lay down my life.

I asked God for His Holy love.
He said to keep His commands.
I asked for wisdom and knowledge.
He said to take a firm stand.

I asked God for living water.
He said to bring Him praise.
I asked for bread from Heaven.
He said to walk in His ways.

I asked for His loving kindness.
He said to be kind to man.
I asked God for His salvation.
He said to obey His plan.

I Came Across

I came across
A stumbling block,
Stumped my toe
Upon a rock.
When I cried out
Cause of the pain,
Jesus cleansed me
Of the stain.
I came across
A path so wide;
And started down it
With great pride.
But when I found
Myself a ditch in,
Jesus helped me
To start again.
I came across
A falling star;
Began to follow
From afar.
But when I found out
Which way he led,

"Follow Me
Jesus said.
I came across
A broken man;
And did not really
Understand;
And did not want
To get involved;
But Jesus said to
His problem solve.

I Can Still Go On

Though I've known rejection;
Though I've known defeat;
Though I've known failure;
Though I've known retreat
I can go on from this place;
I can still go on from here
Knowing Christ Jesus loves me,
And accepts my broken tears.

Though I've known deception;
Though I've known unrest;
Though I've known insecurity
I can still stand the test.
I can go on from this place;
I can still go on from here
Knowing Christ Jesus loves me,
And accepts my broken tears.

I Charge Angels

I charge angels
To go before me
And prepare the way
For the Word of God.
I charge angels
To clear a path
For this messenger
To safely trod.
I charge angels
To soften hearts
Of many a lost soul,
Them to prepare
To receive
A Living Word
That'll spare them from
The flames of eternal Hell.
I charge angels
To keep the way
Safe from the snares
Of the fowler's hand,
So this messenger
Can yield to God

By reaching for
The lost man.
If the enemy
Tries to block
The path of this Messenger,
I charge angels
To use faith to win
In this spiritual war.
Angelic hosts
Look down on us
From Heaven's Holy place
To work for us
On our behalf
Because of Divine grace,
That favor of God
We don't deserve,
But receive unmerited,
Allows these angels
Of the Most High
To fight through Christ's blood
To bring our souls
Back into
Divine grace and favor with Him
So that we
Can know our God
And spend eternity with Him.
Oh what love
Shown toward us

By Christ upon the Cross,
For through His surrender
Unto obedience in death
He did not suffer loss;
But gained a Church
That spanned two centuries
And still it marches on;
But soon the trumpet
Will blow from Heaven
And this Church will then be gone;
So don't be left behind
When this Church flies away;
But make your peace
With Almighty God;
And do it, yes, today.

I Don't Want To Be Too Busy

I want to hear
His still small voice
As He speaks to me.
I don't want to be
Too busy for the Lord
To set me free.
I want to reach out
And touch the Lord
As He passes by.
I don't want to be
Too busy
To hear His tender cry.

I Go To Jesus

Where do I go
When bitterness knocks
Continually upon
My heart's lock
Trying to gain
An entrance here
To fill my life
With pain and fear?

I go to Jesus
In times of prayer,
And ask Him to answer
My times of despair
Through forgiveness, peace,
Joy, and hope.
Through these He'll give me
The means to cope.

What do I say
When anger beckons
For me to seek
Revenge to reckon

To someone for
The hurt they've caused?
Through their selfish intent
My life they've paused.

I go to Jesus
In times of prayer,
And ask Him to answer
My times of despair
Through forgiveness, peace,
Joy, and hope.
Through these He'll give me
The means to cope.

Where do I go
To flee from pain
Caused by life's
Uncertain rain
That daily pours
Upon my soul
In it's attempt
To take control?

I go to Jesus
In times of prayer,
And ask Him to answer
My times of despair
Through forgiveness, peace,
Joy, and hope.
Through these He'll give me
The means to cope.

I'm Looking For The Day

I'm looking for the time.
I'm looking for the day
That Jesus Christ will come
And catch us all away.

I'm listening for the sound.
I'm listening for the call
When Jesus Christ will come
And take us one and all.

I'm listening for the sound,
Oh, that great trumpet sound;
For when that trumpet blows
We will all leave the ground.

We're going to be caught up
In the clouds of glory.
We're going to be caught up
To meet Him in the air.
We're going to be caught up
In the clouds of glory,
Going home to be with Him
Eternity to share.

I Need Forgiveness, Peace, Joy, and Hope

Forgiveness answers
The bitter demands
Of anger's lack
To understand.
Peace can only come
Through simple trust
In the one that knows
Much more than us.
Joy is the fruit
Of the faithful stand
For truth and mercy,
And God's plan.
Hope, my friend,
Anchors the soul
In the presence of Him
That makes us whole.

I Wish You Were Here

Although
You continually
Disregard My Word,
And continue to walk
According to this world,
There is something
I want you to know:
I wish you were here
To enjoy this show.

All of the angels
Surrounding the throne
Dancing and shouting,
Rejoicing over one
Who has just surrendered
And given his life
To My will and purpose
And to walk in My light.

If only you knew
How much you would bless
Should you submit

To this one request:
To repent of all sin,
And walk in My light,
The angels would rejoice
And stand ready to fight
Upon your behalf
To help you to live
According to My purpose,
According to My will.

I wish you were here
To enjoy this great place
Where the streets are gold,
And the rivers are grace,
The walls are all jasper,
The gates are all pearl,
The mansions are all built;
And as prophecy unfurls
I so wish you were here
To enter your peace,
And live forever
In Heaven with Me.

I Would That You Would

I would that you would listen,
And then take earnest heed
To the Word that'll spare you
From the end of sinful deeds.

I would that you would watch
And then carefully beware
Of the enemy's attempts
Your life on Earth to impair.

I would that you'd feel after
And faithfully reach out
To receive the strength you need
To victoriously win each bout.

I would that you would taste
Of My Good Holy Word
By meditating upon
That which you have heard.

I would that you would sense
And learn to discern
The value of My Presence;
In Eternity you'll affirm.

If His Hands

If his hands touch my hands,
Then our hands can PLAY A MELODY.

If his mind becomes my mind,
Then our mind becomes INFINITY.

If his word becomes my word,
Then our word becomes AUTHORITY.

If his life becomes my life,
Then our life becomes ETERNITY.

If his will becomes my will,
Then our will becomes HEAVENLY.

If his faith becomes my faith,
Then our faith becomes VICTORY.

If his love becomes my love,
Then our love can REACH THE LONELY.

If his ways become my ways,
Then our ways become HOLY.

If his thoughts become my thoughts,
Then our thoughts become LOVELY.

If I Bless, Will You?

My child,
If I bless you;
Would you then bless me
By blessing all those
That you come into contact with
Or see;
Or will you just keep My blessing
All to yourself;
And consider it to be
Your own personal wealth?
My blessing, my child,
Is to be shared;
And to be spread around
By all those who care;
Not to be hoarded
And cleaved to the breast,
Or to be clung to;
For, you see.
It is really a test
To see if you're willing
To lay down your life,
And deny yourself of

The cares and the strife.
So, when blessings do come,
Invest them well
In the lives of others
Who then can tell
Of the grace of God
That helped them through
By blessing them with
A friend like you.

If I Love God

If I love God
Because He first loved me
Enough to come and die
On the Cross of Calvary,
Then can my love for Him endure
Much suffering and much pain,
Or will I just buckle
Underneath the strain?

"I am persuaded
That He is able
To keep that
Which I have committed
Unto Him
Against that day."

If Jesus is the author
And the finisher of my faith,
Then I know that I can continue
And endure hardship in this race
All the way to glory
Or the time that He returns
To receive those who are His own
And to see His face they yearn.

If I Were

If I were
To stand apart
And view life from a distance,
Wouldn't I then
Only know
What I would see
Just by its mere appearance?
Would I ever
Get to know
The innermost feelings of life;
Unless I chose
To participate in daily events and strife?

★ ★ ★

If I'd Never

If I'd never
Fought a fight,
Been knocked down,
Whether wrong or right,
I would have never
Found the strength
To run this race,
To run this length.

If I'd never
Struggled with sin,
Resisted temptation,
Again and again,
I would have never
Found the faith
To continue running
in this race.

If I'd never
Felt the pain
Of a heart
That's filled with rain,
I could never fully
Appreciate the peace
And the joys of being
Completely set free.

If You Haven't Yet

If you haven't yet
Made up your mind
With Jesus Christ
New life to find,
It's your future
That you postpone.
If you haven't yet
Taken a firm stand
To walk with God
And follow His plan,
It's your blessing
That you postpone.
If you haven't yet
Decided to get
Ready for His return
You just might find out
You've been left out
With no where else to turn.

So, count the cost
And be sure you know
How much would be lost
If you don't go
When Christ returns
In the air
To claim His own
And His glory share.

If You Only Knew

If you only knew
How short the time,
Would you then speak
To that friend of thine?

Or would you keep
A hold of that
Bitter grudge you
Conceived in spat?

Is it really worth
That ton of guilt
That weighs you down
Causing you to tilt

Your head down low
With solemn face
Finding it so hard
Your guilt to erase?

So, make your peace
While you still can
With that ole Joe,
With your old friend.

I'm Sorry, God

I'm sorry, God,
For this mess I'm in.
It's really all because
I have committed sin
In allowing another master
To lead my soul astray.
I find now that I'm adrift
So very far from the way.

I'm really sorry, God.
I do so want to find
My way back to You
Who is so loving and so kind.
To think that you've waited,
Longing for this very day
That I'd turn again to You
And with humble heart pray.

I'm really very sorry, God.
Will You please forgive
And lead me back again
To the way so that I can live,

For as yet I'm still drowning
In so much debt and despair
That I'm even wondering
If anyone even cares
Whether or not I succeed
Or fail, live or die,
Whether or not I go to Heaven
Or in Hell I fry.

Lord, I need to be wanted
And needed by someone
That longs to be with me
To live and have fun.
I need some help and incentive
To work my way free
From this snare that I'm caught in;
Yes, from this sin disease.
Please forgive, oh Lord,
And help me please to find
My way back to You,
Your presence and peace of mind.

I'm Thankful

I'm thankful that I'm alive.
I'm thankful that I can breathe.
I'm thankful for those things
I've been able to achieve.
I'm thankful for my faith
And those things that I believe.

I'm thankful for this hope.
I'm thankful for God's love.
I'm thankful that all good
And perfect gifts come from God above.
I'm thankful for God's Spirit
That descends upon us like a dove.

I'm thankful for my friends
And precious family
And all those whose influence
Have helped me to be me.
I'm thankful for my God
And my relationship with Him,
From which all the peace and joy
In my life does so richly stem.

I'm thankful for the Cross
Upon which Jesus died,
And for the empty tomb
Left by His resurrection stride.

I'm thankful for the Gospel,
The which I've obeyed.
Through the same I've received the power
That by which my sin was stayed.

In His Hands

In His hands
Are the oceans.
In His hands
Is the breeze.
In His hands
Are the mountains.
In His hands
Are the trees;
And whether or not
We know what
His word has revealed,
In His hands
His future plans
Here-to-fore
Have been concealed.

In His hands
Are the rivers.
In his hands
Are the streams.
In His hands
Are the storms.

In His hands
Are our dreams;
And whether or not
We have come
This to understand,
In His hands,
His future plans
By him
Can be revealed.

In His hands
Are our wants.
In His hands
Are our needs.
In His hands
Are our prayers.
In His hands
Are our pleas;
And whether or not
We know when
He has answered our prayers,
In His hands,
His future plans,
We know that
He is there.

In His hands
Are our losses.
In His hands

Are our gains.
In His hands
Are our chances
That we can
Begin again;
For whether or not
We know what
For us the future holds,
In His hands,
His future plans,
Can then
To us be told.

★ ★ ★

In This Ole Life's Game

When you entertain a stranger,
And he helps you to see
How to climb out of trouble;
And you work your way free;
Could this be an angel
That you have entertained;
Or just another player In this ole life's game?

When your vehicle is broken down
On the side of life's highway;
And you look up to God
Cry out and pray.
Then someone comes along
Just in the nick of time;
And before too very long
You are doing just fine.
Could this be an angel
That you have entertained;
Or just another player
In this ole life's game?
When you're down sick,
And discouraged too;

Wondering if you'll get better,
Or what else you can do;
And someone comes to see you
That you just don't know;
And lifts you up in spirit,
Leaving you all aglow.
Could this be an angel
That you have entertained;
Or just another player
In this ole life's game?

You see,
The Word tells us be careful
Just who we entertain;
It just could be an angel
In this ole life's game.

In Whose Eyes

In whose eyes do you want
To be a winner?
When the Devil
Parades his heroes,
Trying to tell us
Each day,
That if we try
To be like them,
We'll be
A winner one day;
But he always
Shows us his rookies,
Never the skid-row Bum,
Who can't even
Keep himself working,
Because of
A bottle of rum.
He never shows us the man
Addicted to crack cocaine;
Nor does he show us the woman
Walking the streets in shame.
When you follow

The path of those heroes, my friend,
The one thing you won't do
Is the victory win.

When the world
Parades their's before us,
Those who have
Riches and fame,
The one thing that
You can't see is
Their emptiness and their pain;
For riches won't bring you fulfillment.
Fame can't fill up your heart
To keep loneliness from entering,
Or cause emptiness to depart.
But when the witnesses
Start coming to see you
To declare
What Jesus can do,
It usually is not one of His rookies
That's testifying to you
Of all the things
That God has done or will do.
It is usually one that's been
Through all kinds of trials and tests,
And found out that following Jesus
Is the road that really is best.
Whenever you look at His heroes
That are mentioned

Throughout God's word,
They are always
Standing quite firmly;
Their message,
Undeniably heard;
That if you really want
To be a winner,
In His eyes
Is really the place;
For it is there
That you will find
So very much peace and grace.

Infatuation

Infatuation
Is delusive
In its approach to you;
For it usually tells you things
That for the most part
Just aren't true;
Then once your heart is open,
You are really set
To be emotionally hurt
And full of much regret.

True love starts small,
Down deep within the heart;
Then steadily grows
'Til it fills all,
Not just merely a part.
It burns within
Just like a flame
That causes feelings so warm.
It destroys all selfishness
Like a mighty storm.

Where infatuation fleets away
After just a little while;
True love just keeps on flowing
Like the mighty Nile.

While infatuation is built upon
What you just hope is really true;
True love's foundation actually is
No real mystery to you.

Infatuation's the balloon
That's once it's inflated so tight;
While reality is the pin
That brings an end to it's flight.

True love's that little mustard seed
Dropped into the ground;
That once it has fully grown
Covers everything around.

So if you're wondering
Just how that you
Can tell the two apart.
Just wait and see;
For time will tell.
Believe me. That's smart.

Innocent Eyes

Innocent eyes
Peer at life
And cannot see no ill.
They only see
The purity of
A heart full of good will.
They're usually taken
By surprise
When someone does them harm;
For they were not
Taught the signs
To watch for them to warn.
So naive
Are those that peer
At life through innocent eyes.
Many things
That people do
So often takes them by surprise.
So if you're one
That peers through life
Through eyes of innocence
Be careful when

255

You enter into
Relations of romance;
For there are those
Who'll prey on you
If given the slightest chance;
And they'll take you for
All that you have,
And upon your soul they will prance.

Inspiration

Inspiration;
How it comes and goes;
Whenever it comes;
Oh how it flows.
How to tap into it;
Very few know
About inspiration;
How it comes and it goes.

✫ ✫ ✫

Intoxicated

I want to be
Intoxicated with
That precious
Holy Ghost wine;
You know, that stuff
That comes from fruit
Grown upon Jesus
The True Vine.

It'll take you much
Higher than high;
Yet leave you with
No reason to sigh.
It's an experience that
You'll never get over;
And you won't ever wake up
With a bad hang over.

You can get oh so drunk
On this Heavenly brew
That you'll be surprised at
The next thing you do.

But one thing is for certain
You won't have to worry about;
It'll never cause you to do wrong.
Of this there is no doubt.

Don't you want to be
Intoxicated with
That precious
Holy Ghost wine;
You know, that stuff
That comes from fruit
Grown upon Jesus,
The True Vine.

It'll take you
Higher than high;
Yet leave you with
No reason to sigh.
It's an experience
That you'll never get over;
And you won't ever wake up
With a bad hangover.

You can get oh, so drunk
On this Heavenly brew
That you'll be surprised at
At the next thing you'll do.
But one thing is for certain
You won't have to worry about;
It'll never cause you to do wrong;
Of this there is no doubt.

Inward Struggle

There's a battle going on;
And it's raging now within.
It's the flesh against the spirit;
And they both desire to win.
Before I became aware
Of this inward fight,
I continually made decisions
That proved not to be right.
Now as long as I'm aware
That this battle is a-raging,
I can control the outcome
By the choices that I'm making.
If I sit back and relax,
And take this fight for granted,
I'll find myself doing wrong
By this world enchanted.

J's

Walk The Talk
Religious Right Is Not Christian

1PercentRevolution ☽211

Jacob's Eyes

Jacob's eyes
Were on an eternal prize
When he proposed to Esau
To purchase his birthright.
He was really looking
Beyond the here and now,
When he stole the Blessing
Of his father's power.
Then again at Bethel,
Where he wrestled all night
With one of God's Holy angels
With all of his mortal might,
To gain God's Holy blessing
Upon his mortal life,
Not to mention,
Divine protection
From his brother's strife.
Looking far
Beyond his plight,
Wrestling there all the night
For God to be with him
In his homeward flight.

That night
He grabbed a hold of
A treasure hardly told:
The blessing of the Almighty,
All because he was bold.

You see,
Jacob's eyes
Were on an
Eternal prize.

Jesus The Awesome

Jesus, You're so awesome
And so great.
Your ways are so amazing.
The fact that you loved
A wretch like me,
To me is just astounding.
God, there is no one else
That can save me
From the whiles of sin and self,
And set me again
Upon a path
Of spiritual wisdom and wealth.
So, I do praise
And exalt you
As high as I possibly can;
So, that You can
Draw all men to You,
Unto your guiding Hand.

★ ★ ★

Jesus Will Still Be There

There are gonna be some smiles,
There are gonna be some frowns,
There are gonna be some trials.
There are gonna be some crowns;
But whatever life may bring around
Jesus Christ will still be there for you.

What ever life may have brought in,
Jesus Christ will still be your friend.
Whatever this world may bring you through,
Jesus Christ will still be there for you.

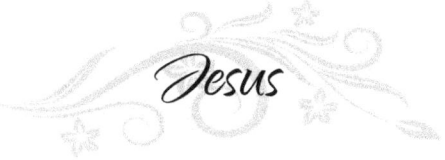

Jesus

"J" is for He's Just
And righteous altogether.

"E" is for He's Eternal;
For He will reign forever.

"S" is for He's our Sacrifice
To redeem our souls from sin.

"U" is for that He Understands
What it takes for us to win.

"S" is for He's our Security;
For in Him we are secure.

And all this spells Jesus,
The name of Christ our Saviour.

Just An Acquaintance

Just an acquaintance,
That's all He tiz.
I met Him while
About my biz.

He called me with
A voice so strong
That I talked with Him
All night long;
And when He left
My company,
Somehow I felt
That I was free.

As I lived
My life awhile,
I noticed Him watching
Me with a smile.
Not a word
Did He speak to me.
Just a longing
In His eyes I'd see.

Although He made
His presence known,
I waited just
A bit too long.
When finally I thought
I'd look His way,
I noticed that
He did not stay.

Just an acquaintance,
That's all He tiz;
So I went on
About my biz.

A day or two
Went by so fast.
I turned and looked;
And there He passed.
I quickly tried
To catch up to Him.
Again too late;
He's getting dim.

Just an acquaintance,
That's all He tiz;
So I went on
About my biz.

A month or two
Went by so fast.

I heard him calling
As I passed;
But too busy
Was I right then.
When I turned and looked;
He was gone again.

Just an acquaintance,
That's all He tiz;
So I went on
About my biz.

A year or two
Went by so fast.
I heard Him crying
As I passed;
"Come unto Me
All ye that labor.
I'll help you through.
I'll be your Saviour."

Just an acquaintance,
That's all He tiz;
So I went on
About my biz.

A decade or two
Went by so fast.
I heard Him weeping
As I passed.

This time I stopped
To take a look;

And caught a glimpse
Of the cross He took.
I saw Him suffering
There for me;
So that I
Might be set free;
And when I
Identified
With His pain,
I had to cry.
Then again,
We talked awhile;
And once more
I saw Him smile.

No more, said I,
Will this Man be
Only an
Acquaintance to me.
I'll seek Him out
Each and everyday.
I'll look to Him;
And I'll pray.

Just How Bad Is Hell Going To Be?

I asked God,
"Just how bad is Hell going to be?"
And this is what He said to me:
"Consider My Word, My child,
That tells you about
How magnificently beautiful
That Heaven will be;
How splendid to be without
Pain or tears,
Sickness or death;
The security of
Walking on streets of gold
And being inside
Those magnificent walls of jasper;
The freedom of having
Twelve huge gates of pearl
From which to come and go;
And after you have imagined Heaven
As great as you can possibly imagine it;
Then consider Hell

As its exact opposite.
Just as unfathomable
As Heaven will be in greatness;
Hell will be
Just as an unfathomably awful place
As Heaven will be great."

Just How Much?

Just how much
Did it cost;
When you broke
That old antique vause;
Or when your
Black sheep got lost;
Or when the wrong
Thing you tossed?

Just how much
Did you lose;
When you did
Not get to snooze;
Or when you ran
Out of booze;
Or when you put your
Head in the noose?

Just how much
Did it really pay;
When you went down
The right way;

Or when you just
Decided to stay;
Or for five more minutes
You just continued to lay?

Just how much
Did you save;
When you waited
For the next wave,
Or when you walked
Out on the pave,
Or when you just
Did not shave?

Just how much
Did it cost;
When your great
Dane got lost,
Or when your credit
Card got tossed,
Or when you slapped
Your old boss?

Please tell me;
Just how much?

Just One Chance

How about a chance, oh life,
To make my mark on you,
To affect the lives of people,
And to help them make it through,
To change the course of history,
And spare this nation from
The disaster that it's headed for
Due to the beating of sin's drum.
JUST ONE CHANCE
Is all I ask,
For that is all I'll need
To become
In this final hour
Of revival, just a seed.

How about a chance, oh life,
To reach for higher goals,
To help finance revival
In this world of lost and dying souls,
To create a spark
That would ignite
Holy fire that would consume

The sacrifices of Holy Saints,
While bringing souls forth from their womb.
JUST ONE CHANCE
Is all I ask,
For that is all I'll need
To become
In this final hour
Of revival, just a seed.

How about a chance, oh life,
To see my dreams come true
Of helping train an army
Of Christians soldiers who
Would storm this world
With His power through God's Holy name,
And bring forth a revival
Of an unquenchable flame.
JUST ONE CHANCE
Is all I ask,
For that is all I'll need
To become
In this final hour
Of revival, just a seed.

Just What Is It That Are You After?

Eve was after the forbidden fruit;
Cain was after acceptance;
Enoch was after God's pleasure;
Noah was after salvation;
My friend, what are you after?
Abraham was after an eternal inheritance;
Sarah was after a promise child;
Jacob was after Divine blessing;
Esau was after a bowl of pottage;
My friend, what are you after?
Joseph was after a dream;
Moses was after the law;
Israel was after the promised land
While they chased after the cloud;
My friend, what are you after?
Rahab was after deliverance;
Joshua was after the captain of the host of Israel;
King Saul was after some donkeys;
King David was after God's heart;
My friend, what are you after?

King Solomon was after Divine wisdom
While he pursued his every desire;
Daniel was after Divine favor
While the kings of Babylon were after World domination;
My friend, what are you after?
Hosea was after the love of a harlot
While in pursuit of his wayward children;
The disciples were after Christ's teachings
To understand His miraculous ways;
My friend, just what is it that are you after?
The Apostle Paul told us in Romans 8
Just how we can make our pursuit prosperous
Is not in that we produce the right works,
But it is just in what we are after.

Just Who?

Just who can I win?
Who can I win to You, Lord?
Please open my ears
So, I can hear Your Word;
Then open my eyes
That I may see
The face of that soul
I can win to Thee.
If my life
Cannot yet count
And impact some soul
That upon my life would mount
A trophy of grace,
A jewel so rare,
That my crown in heaven
Would have a bright glare.
I'm not looking
For rewards down here
Upon this dusty old
Earthly sphere;
But if I could
Just hear You say, "Well done";

Then I'd feel like
I really have won.
Just who can I touch
With a word today?
Just who can I effect
With something I'd say?
Just who can I reach
By what I would do?
Oh how can my life
Be pleasing to You?
What can I do
To reach some soul;
So that You Lord
Can make them whole.
Please open my eyes
That I can see.
Sometimes,
I feel like I'm blinded
By my view of me.

K's

Kindness

"K" is for it's the KEY
To being well thought of.

"I" is for it's the IDEAL BEHAVIOR
Towards the ones you love.

"N" is for that NEVER
Should you let this attitude slip from you.

"D" is for the DIFFERENCE
You'll experience should you ever do.

"N" is for how NICE
You feel when people to you are kind.

"E" is for the ENCOURAGEMENT you feel
When you keep them in mind.

"S" is for how S*ACRED*
Your memories of their kindness are.

"S" is for your sacrifice of K*INDNESS*
Can help you win your internal war.

L's

Laughter

Laughter is a medicine
That'll cure so many ills.
It'll do a better job
Than so many of our pills.
Jesus is the physician
That prescribes this medicine.
The Holy Ghost is the pharmacist
That'll fill this prescription.
So, when our life is filled
With sorrow and despair,
If we'll visit Doctor Jesus
Though the medium of prayer;
And once we have repented
Of our arrogance and pride;
Perhaps a little laughter
Is what He will prescribe.

★ ★ ★

Lead The Way

Lord, I know
That there are trials
That I have yet to face
And with Your help
I'll breeze through them
Like a runner in a race;
Although I know
That should I turn
From this Spirit-led way
I'll face some things
You do not intend
To spring up in my way;
So Lord, here I am
All ready to give in
To follow after
Your every move
And through You eternally win;

And that's the reason
I'm sitting here
As I humbly pray.
I need You, Lord,
To go before
And to lead the way.

Learn Your Lessons

When troubles come,
And you're not sure
If you will ever
Find a cure
That will level
The playing field
'Til you can compete
Instead of yield,
Do you just
Throw in the towel,
Or learn through them
Like the wise old owl.
Once you learn
These lessons that come
Through troubles and through trials
You will soon
Be able to
Go through life with a smile;
For life may twist
And life may turn,
But it is so that
We can then learn,

And stretch and grow,
And then mature
Into men and women
That can stand sure.

Let Christ Be Your Patch

At times it's hard
To trust the Lord
When your dreams
Don't His match.
You feel as though
You'll loose your dreams
And your life will need a patch.
So, you kick and scream
To keep your dreams.
You even claw and scratch,
Until you stop
And recognize
The Almighty has no match.
So, do you give in
And yield to Him
His will then to catch?
His way is best.
You'll find peace and rest,
And Christ will be your patch.

Let This Light So Shine

How can I just sit
And watch a world go astray?
How can I stand by
While millions are held at bay?
How can I just not do
What God has called me to?
How can I love God
If I can't prayerfully love you?
No, I cannot sit Idly by;
While this world spins
Its way to Hell.
I cannot let
Myself stand still;
While millions
Just scream and yell.
I can't continue
To hesitate
To heed this Gospel call;
But I must prove
My love for God
By loving one and all.
I must stand in the gap,

And form a bridge
With my fervent prayer,
Showing everyone I meet
How much my God cares.

I must now step out by faith,
And do those things
That I'm afraid to do,
If I'm ever going to prove
That my love for God is true.
I must walk in the light,
And let God reveal
Those things that hinder me;
So that my worship
Of my Lord
Can be set completely free.
This world must see
A man of God
Completely given to Him,
Not held back
From God's will
By some earthly whim.
They must see
A shining light
In answer to God's call.
One that will direct
The steps of many,
And lift up the souls that fall.
They must see

A man that's empty
Of His own selfish desires,
That's been set aflame
With the love of God,
And with Holy Ghost fire.

It's not enough
To just stand by,
And watch from the side line;
But I must plunge
Into the fight,
And let this light so shine.

Let Us Choose

Just where would I be
Without His mercy?
And without His Truth
Can anyone actually be free?
For until you know Truth
You have no choice
But to walk in error;
And until you experience mercy,
All you have to look forward to
Is judgment.
We all are recipients of
His long suffering,
While He waits for us to choose.
Will it be Truth,
Or error?
Mercy,

Or Judgment?
What about me?
What about you?
Let us choose.

Life Can Be Cruel

Life can be so cruel.
It can really be so mean.
It can wreck all your plans;
And squelch all your dreams.
It can spin you round in circles
So that you don't even know
Just exactly where you are.
It can cause you to wonder
If there's even a chance
That you can win this war.

But though life to you becomes
Like a raging storm;
There is someone that can help;
And will be there when you mourn.
He'll reach down in your brokenness;
And pick up all your pieces;
And pour out the Balm of Gilead
To bring you new releases.

Life Goes On

Although life may twist and life may turn,
And the plans you make may just burn
In the ashes of broken promises
Of those you've loved and those you've kissed;
You can rebuild upon the foundation
Of new beginnings if you insist;
For if you adopt a determination
To survive your degradation
You can arise up from these ashes,
And be healed of your wounds and gashes.
For life goes on, and on it goes;
No matter what hinders; no matter who knows;
And until God in Heaven says, "Enough!",
Life will continue, whether easy or tough.

Life Is Full Of Blessings

Life is full of blessings
That we often fail to see;
When we're greeted with a smile
By some stranger that we meet;
When a child wants to know you
And desires to draw you in
To their little world
To make of you their new friend;
When this family seems to see you
And let you know they care
By then speaking to you,
"How are you doing there?"

Life is so full of blessings
That we often fail to see,
Flowers that come in bloom,
A singing bird in a tree,
The pets that do so love us,
And families that do care.
Most of us do have someone
That we can then life share.

Just because we miss them
Through the busy-ness of life
Does not mean they don't exist
In the midst of daily strife.
Sometimes we need
To just slow down
So that we can see
The blessings that fill
Our lives each day
For God loves to meet our need.

Lonely

"*L*" *is for the* LONGING
For the fellowship of a friend.

"*O*" *is for this* OBVIOUS
Void that is within.

"*N*" *is for the* NEED *that*
You feel within your soul.

"*E*" *is for this* EXAMINATION
Of why you cannot feel whole.

"*L*" *is for these* LESSONS *that you*
Learn through having this feeling.

"*Y*" *is for the* YEARNING
To be with friends congealing.

Lonesome?

Lonesome days
And lonesome nights
Can seem so empty
And void of light,
Unless you know
The God above,
Who can fill that void
With His peace and love;
But even then
You may not win;
For you must then
Invite Him in;
And should you do
You'll surely find
A loving God
And peace of mind.

Look To Jesus

When what to do
Is not real clear;
And your nerves
Are knotting up with fear;
And it's all you can do
To hold back the tear;
Look to Jesus.
He will help you find the way.

When the answers are just
Too hard for you to find;
And you have just got
Too much on your mind;
And if only you could
Just relax and unwind;
Look to Jesus.
He will help you find the way.

When you are lonely,
And feeling blue;
Others have just
Been untrue to you;

And there is so much left
For you to do;
Look to Jesus.
He will help you find the way.

When life has dealt
To you a bad hand;
And there are some things
You just don't understand;
And you feel you are standing
In a strange land;
Look to Jesus.
He will help you find the way.

When you are sick,
Longing to get well;
The last time you felt good
Is hard for you to tell;
And you just feel like
Giving out a loud yell;
Look to Jesus.
He will help you find the way.

Looking At Calvary

Looking at Calvary,
What do I see,
Through all the suffering,
And pain, and agony?
I see love and hate.
I see destiny and fate.
I see satisfaction and contentment.
I see anxiety and resentment.
I see the ugliness of sin;
And yet, God's beauty in men.
Looking at Calvary,
What do I see,
Through all the darkness, and death;
What is the key?
I see war and peace.
I see sickness and health.
I see rejection and acceptance.

I see poverty and wealth.
I see sin as defeated
Through surrender's victory;
Because Jesus won that battle
In Gethsemane.

Looking For Love

Carefully,
Looking for love.
Wondering who
Might care enough
To risk
Exposing themselves,
Their inner self.
To love Is to risk
Being hurt.
It actually hurts
To love.
But love also
Brings happiness.
In fact
The hurts of love
And its happiness
Are always extreme.

The question is,
Is the happiness of love
Worth the risk
Of the hurts of love?
God thought so.

Lord, Be My Umbrella

Lord, I know
That this rain
That's falling all around
Is so necessary to life;
So, I'm not asking
For this rain to stop;
Just help me with the strife.
Now Lord, I may be tired,
And do not really
Care to be drenched;
But I do so desire
That through this rain
This long drought be quenched.
So, I'm not asking
For this rain to quit;
Just be my umbrella, oh Lord,
And keep me from getting wet.
Lord, let this rain
Continue to pour;
Cause all that are around here
Really do need it more.
Just let your grace

Spread out its wings;
And cover my life during this storm.
"Be my umbrella,"
Is what I sing
While this my strength is worn.

Lord Bless This Mess

Lord bless this mess
That I must eat;
And make it taste
So good and sweet;
And bless the hands
That made this mess;
And let them know
That they are blessed.

★ ★ ★

Lord, Cleanse Me

Lord, cleanse my mind
With Your Word.
Help me heed
To what I've heard.
Lord, cleanse my soul
Of what it's wrought,
And help me live
By what You've taught.

Lord, cleanse my mind
With Your Blood.
Wash my soul
'Neath the crimson flood.
Lord, here's my heart.
Cleanse every part,
And Lord please,
Give to me
A brand new start.

Lord, How Much Do I Love You?

Lord, How much do I love You?
Let me count the ways.
I love You so very much,
That I'll give You all the praise.
And as I live this life,
I'll do my very best to
Live it in such a way
That it will be pleasing to you.

✬ ✬ ✬

Lord, I Have To Crucify This Old Man Again

Lord, there are some things within me
I need to put to death.
Yes, there are some desires within me
I need to put to death.
Lord, I need
To crucify
This old man again
If I'm ever
Going to
The victory win.
Lord, I need
To tell this old man
"You have to die today.
Just step back
And let the Lord
Have His own way."

★ ★ ★

Lord, I want

Lord, I want
To abide in You,
And for your Word
To abide in me.
Lord, I want
To do Your will
More than I want You
To do the will of me.
It doesn't matter
If I receive
Whatsoever that I ask;
For what matters most
Is that I know
That to me
You're not just a mask.

I desire Your presence
Within my life
To be a stark reality.
And to worship your precious name
I desire to be at liberty.

Lord, Why?

Lord,
Why is it so hard
To climb over this wall
That I have allowed to grow
Oh, so very tall?

Am I so afraid
That I might just slip,
Loose my hold, and fall;
Or is it because I lack the faith,
And don't believe in myself at all?

Lord,
You know that I
Desire not to dwell alone.
Oh, if I could just have
A friend to talk to
On the phone.

I'm trying to live
In such a way that
Would be pleasing to You;
And by Your grace

I have kept myself
Morally clean and pure.
Haven't I yet proved
To be faithful enough
For You to bless me with a wife;
Or is it really
Your perfect will for me
To remain single
The rest of my natural life?

Well Lord,
I'm not really mad
Or angry at You at all.
I just wish
That Your will
Was much easier to find,
That's all.

Lord, You Are Welcome To Interrupt Me

Lord, you are welcome
To interrupt my life;
Especially, Lord, when I'm
In the midst of strife.
You're welcome to enter in
Any time that you please.
Lord, you are welcome
To interrupt me.

Love (A)

"L" is for the LONGING
Of the One True God
For someone with which to walk
And with Him through eternity trod.

"O" is for His OMNIPOTENCE
By which He created this world
When He spoke it all into existence
Causing His Word to be unfurled.

"V" is for the VIBRANCY
Of His Awesome Holy Presence
As He first walked with Adam
In the garden of His essence.

"E" is for ETERNITY
Which is what He wants to share
With those that choose to live for Him
With a life that's filled with care.

Love

Some say that love is blind;
But I say love can see
Much farther and much deeper
Than the naked eye can see.
Love can see the brokenness
Of one's spirit in a cry.
Love can see the remorse
Through the tear
That dims the eye.
Love can see real character
Before it is even conceived.
Love can see a saint
Before that soul's ever believed.
Love can look beyond
All our mistakes and all our faults.
Love can look inside a heart
That is locked up like a vault.
Love can see the joy
That's hidden behind the Cross.
Love can see the victory
On the other side of loss.
Love can see

The freedom of spirit
That comes as one's flesh has been bound.
And love can see the spiritual bondage
When carnal freedom is then found.

Love, Giving, And Living

Love;
Love is of God;
For God is love;
And Jesus was,
And now the church is
The embodiment of love.

Giving
Is the expression
Of love;
For God so loved
That He gave.

Living Is the result
Of giving;
For giving
Is the true reason
For living.

Love Is Greater

Love is greater
Than faith or hope,
For without love
In darkness you'll grope.
And faith is worked
By the love you hold,
And will keep you warm
And out of the cold.
And love gives birth
To hope you see.
And that's why it's greater
Than both of these.

★ ★ ★

Love the Lord

Love the Lord
With all your heart,
And He will give you
A brand new start.
Love the Lord
With all your soul,
And He will make you
Completely whole.
Love the Lord
With all your mind,
And revelation
You will find.
Love the Lord
With all your might,
And He will
Your battles fight.

Make Your Peace With God

Stormy days
And stormy nights
Can fill our hearts
So full of fright,
If we have not
Made our peace with God.

Troubles that come
Into our life
Can fill our hearts
So full of strife,
If we have not
Made our peace with God.

When we face Anxiety,
We'll wonder how
We could get free,
If we have not
Made our peace with God.

When we live
Unto our self,
We'll never find
Eternal wealth,
Until we have
Made our peace with God.

Making Peace

Making peace
Can be real hard
And keeping it
Even harder,
Unless it's between
God and man
Which process
Cannot be simpler;
For Jesus Christ
Paid the price
To eradicate our sin.
If we'll accept
And then obey
Our new life can begin.

Without this gift
That Christ gave
True peace
We will not find.
But once received
You won't believe
How His peace
Will make you shine.

Manly Confession

As a man,
I must confess
That I desire
To you undress;
But as a follower
Of Jesus Christ,
I must not obey
This lustful eye;
For should I do,
I'll find much more
Than what my mind
Had bargained for.

I'll find this fire
That would burn within
With the flame of
Desire to sin;
So let me turn
My eyes from this
Before the righteous
Way I miss.

Meditations

Meditating on
The troubles of this life
Can greatly increase
Your internal strife,
Until you have built
Around yourself a cage;
And then find it so very hard
To even turn the page.

Meditating on
The blessings that God sends
Can greatly increase
A strong faithful trend,
Until you surround yourself
With so much joy and bliss;
Because you are so grateful
For all of God's wonderful gifts.

Memorials

When I remember
The by-gone-days,
Battles fought,
Victories won;
I often find
Myself amazed;
For many times
In days gone by,
I thought the end
Was just in sight;
Only to find
God intervened;
And made a way
I had not seen.

On these times
I dare not dwell
Too very long,
Lest I fail
To see the way
I need to go
To continue on

This Heavenward road;
But just from them
Glean some faith
To help me
Run in this race.

Messiah

"M" is for the MAJESTY
Of the King of kings.

"E" is for the ETERNAL REALM
From which He reigns.

"S" is for His SUFFERING
Through which He paid the price.

"S" is for the SALVATION
Which I enjoy tonight.

"I" is for the INCREDIBLE POWER
Of Jesus blood and name.

"A" is for the AUTHORITY He gives
Over both sin and shame.

*"H" is for His HOLINESS
That His life displayed;*

*For He was MESSIAH
Who gave His life
For ours in trade.*

Mistakes

When we first consider
How much a mistake costs;
We can only think
Of what we've lost;
Then usually we
Just feel such pain;
'Til we consider
Just what was gained.
Oh how big
The minus is to us;
When compared to the first
That was just;
But when this minus
Is taken to heart;
It can reap for us
A brand new positive start.
For when we take to heart
Each mistake that is made;
And learn a better way;
Then we really get paid;
For the lessons in life,
What we from them learn,

Far greatly outweigh
What we could have earned.
But if learn we do not;
And God has to send
Another trial of our faith;
That costs us again.

Mitzy

"M" is for how MILITANT
She is in prayer.

"I" is for how INVOLVED
She is in care.

"T" is for the TRUTH
She loves to proclaim.

"Z" is for her ZEAL
For Jesus NAME.

"Y" is for her YEARNING
By God to be used.

All of this spells "MITZY"
Who has higher things in view.

Mother

"M" is for MERCIFUL;
That's what she's been to me.

"O" is for OBSERVANT;
For there is nothing she doesn't seem to see.

"T" is for TRUSTWORTHY;
For there's nothing she can't be told.

"H" is for her HELPFULNESS;
That is more precious than gold.

"E" is for her ENERGETIC CALL;
That her children will always hear.

"R" is for her REVERENCE FOR GOD;
That motivates her children to fear.

Mother Of Seven

There was this woman
Who had seven daughters,
Some land,
Some horses,
Which could be led
Without halters.
She worked two jobs,
And then sometimes three;
Just to feed
All of this
Great company.
She'd pray for strength,
And daily provision;
While daily facing
A thousand decisions.
Though in her own eyes
A failure;
Others see her as
A woman of great character.
She sees herself as
Always on the edge;
Yet others see her

Just keeping her pledge.
Though in her own eyes
A prisoner
Of responsibility;
Seven daughters watch her
Perform a Queen's liberty.
She'll never know of all
The lives she has touched
Until we're all together
In eternity.

Move Out

Move out from your position
And take the land before you.
Move out from your position.
Your inheritance is there.
Don't stay in your complacency.
Leave the old behind you.
Move out from your position
In the name of the Lord.

Mr. Cain

Sin had left a crimson stain
In the life of Mr. Cain.
Although he thought he had much to gain,
He afterwards really felt the pain.
Oh, Mr. Cain,
Why did you sin again?
Is it because you love the pain;
Or because your in the wrong lane?
Did you think that there was still much to gain;
Or because when it pours, it rains?
Oh Mr. Cain,
Why did you sin again?
God's word to you was very plain;
Yet you rebelled and sinned again.

You've heaped upon yourself
A very great stain
When you disobeyed the Lord and sinned again.
So, Mr. Cain,
Your final lot is real plain;
Because authority you did disdain,
And spent your life in the wrong lane.

Mr. Hope

Mr. Hope,
Where did you go?
Did you fly out the window;
Or walk out the door?
When the bills piled up
And procrastination set in;
When discouragement forced its entrance
And defeat began to win;
Just where can I look
To find you, Mr. Hope;
And how can I deal with life?
Without you, just how can I cope?
When life shakes me silly
Until I can't even tell
Whether I'm standing firm
Or swimming in a well,
Just where will you be?
If I may ask,
Without you, just how will I ever be free?

Music

Music is
The sound of ministry
Though you play and sing
Of God or of the world.
Music ministers
Either life or death,
Morality or immorality,
Good or evil,
right or wrong.
All the same, it ministers.
It supports,
Emphasizes,
Even illuminates
The message of a song;
Which determines it's direction;
Whether it is right or wrong.
Music gives the message
A sort of backbone.

The direction can be
Either heaven or hell,
Faith or sin,
Love or lust,
Life or death;
But all the same,
It just ministers.

My Christmas Wish

In this season
Of the celebration of
Christ I wish to discover
My woman, my wife;
For as yet my life
Is not yet fulfilled,
Nor completed by
A help meet still.
Lord, I'm about
To cross a line,
Not sure if
You think its fine
For me to seek
Outside the Church
To find a bride
Through a worldly search.
If she is near
Yet to be revealed,
Please, let her speak up
My heart to heal.
This move that I'm
About to make

Could very well happen today.
Lord, I know you're still in control
And intend the best
For this my soul;
But this lonely heart

Can't take much more
Of this waiting for
A mate for my soul.
P.S. Lord, please hurry!

My Guardian Angel

No one knows me
Like my GUARDIAN ANGEL;
And, oh,
How he must
Know me!
Oh the things
I put him through;
And all the misery!
Oh how I take
So many chances;
And yet he's still out there;
Standing patient;
Taking glances;
It's how he shows he cares.
Yet one day
When I leave this world,
I think his job will be o'er;
But still I know
my GUARDIAN ANGEL
Will stand by me some more.

So here's to you
my ANGEL;
For all the things you've done;
And please be patient
As you keep me from danger;
Remember,
I'm just a little one.

My Hardest Decision

There is a decision that
I find very hard to make.
It's one where the choices
Are all so very good;
But it'd be so easy to make a mistake.
Any one of these roads
Might be a benefit to me;
But there is only one
That'll ensure liberty.
So, counting the cost
In a situation like this
Can be a real task,
And make it easy to miss,
And cause one to stray from the path
Of the narrow and the straight.
Oh, and how I would love
To see those Pearly Gates.
To only have the wisdom
To know the right way;
Yes, God given discretion not to go astray.
In counting the cost,
Lord, help me to weigh

And measure each and every thought;
So I can see it Your way;
Not to see my life from
Self-centered perspectives of man;
But from the Eternal perspective
One more time again.

My Heart Shall Rejoice

After visiting the halls of deception,
And walking down the corridors of defeat;
After all the bondage is over,
And the enemy has been put in retreat;
My heart shall rejoice in God's mercy;
My tongue shall sing of His grace;
My hands shall applaud His great kindness;
His Holy name I shall praise.

While victory is within my clutches,
And I cling to the God of all ages;
While anointing is flowing within me,
And the Lion of Judah still rages;
My heart shall rejoice in God's mercy;
My tongue shall sing of His grace;
My hands shall applaud His great kindness;
His Holy name I shall praise.

While God's joy is flooding me with strength,
And I'm basking in mercy divine;
When His presence completely assures me
That I'm absolutely connected to the vine;

My heart shall rejoice in God's mercy;
My tongue shall sing of His grace;
My hands shall applaud His great kindness;
His Holy name I shall praise.

When I find myself in the valley
Far from the shout of the mountain
Walking across the great desert of life
Searching for a drink from the fountain;
My heart shall rejoice in God's mercy;
My tongue shall sing of His grace;
My hands shall applaud His great kindness;
His Holy name I shall praise.

My Pastors: Anthony And Mickey

Twenty-five years,
Oh, what a life;
Filled with much love and joy
Along with many tears and strife.
We've walked this road together
Doing God's Holy work,
Pulling people from the mire,
And sinners from the murk,
Preparing them for Heaven,
Getting them ready to fly;
For Jesus soon is coming.
Soon, He'll part the eastern sky.

Twenty-five years,
Oh, what a time.
Thanks be to Jesus
We've let His light so shine.
It has shone out in the gutters.
It has shone out in the streets;
And even in the White House
Before each step of our feet.
We have walked on in His light

And found such love and peace,
And shared it all with others,
So they could find release.

Twenty-five years,
How they've come and gone.
And oh, our faith in God
Has never been so strong;
For all that we have seen
Of God's glorious grace
Has carried us higher and higher
Assuring us a place
Within God's Book of Life
And His Kingdom there.
So, we'll just keep on living
This life of joy and care;
For if God tarries some more
And we are still alive,

I cannot even imagine
What God will do
In the next twenty-five.

My Prayer For Mercy

Oh Lord,
Please don't give me
What I truly deserve;
For how can I
Ever testify
Of the benefits that come
From living a life to You serve?
I realize that I
Have made enough mistakes
To bury any good I've done
With an unrighteous fate;
But please, Lord, look deeper
Than the deeds that I have done,
And have mercy upon
This unrighteous one
By granting a repentance
Not to be repented of,
Then fill this my soul
With Your Divine love
That'll cause me to love
First and foremost, You
So much that I would change

The very things that I would do;
Then to love my neighbor
Much more than myself,
So much that I would be concerned
With their spiritual health;
Then teach me to love
And rejoice in Your truth
Much more than I did
During the times of my youth.
Help me to hate
The deeds of my ways
That has brought me so much grief
That my life is now a maze.
So, please Lord, I beg You,
Help me to repent,
Turning wholly unto You
On this very day;
And let it work
Such a deep work within
That'll completely destroy
Any desire to serve sin.

Don't let me stop short
Of a completed work;
For I don't even want to
Desire with sin to flirt.
Lord, I give You this day
To stand between me
And the ways of sin;
For I really do desire
To start all over again.

My Reasons

LORD, YOUR LIFE is my reason for living.
YOUR GIFT is my reason for giving.
YOUR LOVE is my reason for loving.
YOUR WORK is my reason for working.
YOUR PLAN is my reason for reaching.
YOUR WORD is my reason for preaching.
YOUR LIGHT is my reason for seeing.
AND WHAT YOU ARE is my reason for being.

☆ ☆ ☆

N's

Not Pretending, But Hoping

Lord, You know I don't pretend
To be righteous in all my ways;
But I do really love you
And have for most of my days.
So, if you'll hear this solemn prayer
Offered in humbleness,
I pray forgive my sin,
Wash me within;
For I hope in your mercy and grace.

★ ★ ★

Nothing To Fear

Many times I felt
I could not perform
The task which was at hand;
But when I felt
The good Lord's nudge
Moving me with His hand,
I jumped right in
And did the thing
As if I knew all along.
But it wasn't me,
It was His anointing,
You see.
That's what made me strong.

So now I trust
I can do all things
As long as He is near;
For He's helped me
To truly see
Through Him
There's nothing to fear.

Number One Priority

Just how important to me
Is having Your presence
In my life, oh Lord?
Certainly more important
Than owning that ole Ford;
Or owning my own business,
And having a wife and children;
More that having fame,
Owning my own place or fortune;
More that financial independence,
Or the presence of family;
For without Your presence, oh Lord,
My life is filled with vanity.
Life is just not worth living
Unless You are in it giving
Faith, purpose, and direction,
And are there to give me correction.

Yes, there are some things
That I desire in life;
But, Lord, not if it cost me
My relationship with You,
The Giver Of All Life.

O's

Obstacles

The reality of life,
More often than not,
My squelch a man's dreams
If not his dreams stop.
Whenever he finds
The obstacles so large
It makes it real hard
Good decisions to forge;
But should he take time
To build his dreams up,
He'll then find out
Life's not all that tough.

✰ ✰ ✰

Oh Crown

Oh crown, oh crown,
Oh corruptible crown,
Why doth thou call my name?

Is it to fill
Up my life
With much sin and shame?

To press toward a mark
Down here on earth
Of fortune or of fame?

Oh crown, oh crown,
Oh corruptible crown,
Why doth thou call my name?

Oh crown, oh crown,
Oh corruptible crown,
Why doth thou toll thy bell?

Is it to snag
This ole sinners life
And drag him down to Hell?

Or is it to teach
This poor man lessons
That only time can tell?

Oh crown, oh crown,
Oh corruptible crown,
Why doth thou toll thy bell?

Oh God, I Seek

Oh God, I seek forgiveness for
All the things that I've done
That grieve your heart and make you want
To from my life depart.

Oh God, I seek direction in
This my desolate life
How that I may please You again
And receive Your help with strife.

Oh God, I seek Your face that I
May know just how You feel
About those things
You love the most
So I can serve You with zeal.
Oh God, I seek to know the path
That You will choose for me
For I'm convinced within my heart
Your path will set me free.

Oh God, I seek an open door
Through which I can now walk
And find Your power and the strength

To my old ways then depart.
Oh God, I seek to love You more
Than I ever have before
And once I do I'll even seek
To love You all the more.

On The Edge Of Life

On the edge of life,
Ready to give in,
But cannot find the way
Or even the desire to win.
What is one to do
When all efforts have failed?
Throw in the towel,
Or just go to jail?
I have really tried
Again, and again, and again;
But things just haven't worked out
And desire has really wained.
What is one to do
When he doesn't want to go on?
Give up in despair,
Or pretend and just put on?
I know that God is able
To defeat any foe,
But when one stops his fighting,
Will he the victory know?
On the edge of life,
Fallen to the wind

Of the cares of life
That have mounted and now blend,
Laying there just wounded,
Without direction or desire,
Feeling so inadequate,
In need of spiritual fire.
What is one to do
When he no longer wants to be
Fighting for only survival,
Much less to be free?

One
Is what
We ought to be;
For God is one,
Not two or three.
And when we come
Together in Christ,
We should be united
Through His life.
When division comes,
It's not the Lord;
But it's another
Who is
Tainting the word;
But when revealed,
We can only see
The power of Christian
Unity.

Open Up Your Heart

Open up your heart,
And let Jesus in;
And your life will never
Be the same again.
Listen to His voice,
Harken to His call;
For Jesus will be
Your all in all.

Optical Illusions

Optical illusions present to us pictures that just aren't so. So, when we see an optical illusion, we find that reality is not as it appears to be. What appears to be real is not; and what appears not to be real is. Sometimes people are as optical illusions. On the surface, they appear to be genuine; but once you dig down deep into the heart, they just aren't as they appear to be. Sometimes they appear to be phony on the outside; but, come to find out, they are genuine as pure gold. For this reason, Jesus looks upon the heart. He doesn't judge by the outward appearance. Though a man may appear to be a beggar outwardly; he could very well be a king on the inside. Another man may appear to be rich by outward standards; yet poor when you measure him up to godly standards. A man may appear to be sick unto death by earthly standards; but getting ready to be made whole and complete by heavenly standards. For when you view through these old earthly eyes, you can only view things according to earthly standards; but when you view through heavenly eyes, you have an opportunity to see things by heavenly standards. You might say, "How can I view through heavenly eyes?" Well, you pray for the God of Heaven to open your eyes to the heavenly. Then open your eyes to receive what God will show you. You will find that

God is more willing to reveal the truth to us than we are to see it. For truth will cut away the spiritual cancers. Truth is the pin that pops our illusive balloons. Truth is the light that illuminates our darkness. Optical illusions can only be revealed by the introduction of truth. When truth is received, deception fleets away. When truth is loved, deception cannot find its way back into the heart, though it may seek diligently. A deep abiding love for the truth seals off all the inroads that deception once had into our hearts. This love for the truth will protect us from the optical illusions of spiritual darkness in our day. The scripture teaches us (in the book of Romans) that if a man receives not this love for the truth, that God Himself shall send a strong delusion so that man should believe a lie and be lost. This is also proclaimed in the Kings and Chronicles of the Old Testament; where Macaiah the prophet was sent to King Ahab to tell him that God was sending a lying spirit into the mouths of all the false prophets. Then Ahab followed the council of these false prophets and died in battle. Had Ahab received a love for the truth in his heart, although God Himself sent a strong delusion, this love for truth would have been the shield that protected his heart from believing the lie. But because he did not love the truth, the deception came and swept him away. You see, truth is that two-edged sword of the Spirit that divides and makes the distinction between soul and spirit, good and evil, right and wrong. Our love for truth is our grip on that Sword. You can hold truth with a fish grip or a death grip. And how you love truth will determine how you hold truth, whether or not truth can be wrestled from you.

If your love for truth is a fish grip, then you just might drop it, or it just may be taken from you with little or no effort by the enemy. But if you have a death grip on truth, then nothing will be able to take it from you. Consider that one of King David's Mighty Men fought against the Philistines with such a grip on his sword that men had to pry it out of his hands after the battle. That's how we should hold (love) truth. And if we can hold truth in this way, then we will not fall for the spiritual optical illusions of our day.

Options

You and me,
We have some options,
A choice of mere three,
When it comes to our friends and Hell,
And its certainty.

We can warn them before
With great hope they'll prepare;
So that our friends will surely know
How to avoid going there.

We can arrive on the scene
When that death angel is then nigh;
And hopefully pull them out
Before any of them die.

Or, we can just remain indifferent,
Impervious to this hope;
And forget that God has placed
Into our hands
A rope.

Outside The Grasp

I know the enemy's trying
To get me off track,
And possibly to cause me
To even turn back;
But I know
One thing is sure,
And of this I am certain,
That God will eventually
Punish those
That stay outside the curtain;
So, it is my intention
To press beyond the veil
And stay outside the grasp
Of both sin and Hell.
Though he sends his armies
To combat my stance;
Though he tempt me with success
Of money or romance;
Though he lure me
With the promise
Of power with men through fame;
I'll stay outside the grasp

385

Of the sinful domain.
I'll fight with faith in God
Who is my defense indeed.
I'll share my testimony
And continually plant that seed.

I'll plead the blood of Christ
To cover my soul and life.
I'll stay outside the grasp
Of both sin and strife.

Overcoming Satan's Tricks

If you become sensual
In all of your ways;
Then Satan's tricks
With your mind
He can play;
Because through the senses of the flesh
Does this deceiver work the best.
He'll get you all worked up
Over something that is not;
And although you may know
That it's part of his plot;
You'll play along with his lie for awhile;
Until revealed is
The purpose of his guile.
But should you decide
To fast and to pray;
And to deny
Yourself in this way;
To be deceived
You just will not be
Just as easy as
One, two, three;

For when you silence
The voice of the flesh,
It's easier to determine the sound of the rest;
For the desires of the flesh
Will not taint the sound;
And you'll be surprised
When you've won this round.
The Word says that the Truth
Will set you free.
That also means that the lie
Could bind you, you see.
So if you'll fast and pray
And then read His Word;
You will find that the Truth
By you can be heard;
And to be the victim
Of old Satan's tricks
Won't be your lot
For you gave him your licks.
Victory will be found
Through this method above;
And also you'll find
God's grace and God's love.

Overtime

The Devil's working
Overtime
Motivating people
To commit crime;
Manipulating many
To rebel and fight,
And stubbornly want
Their own way tonight.
He knows his end
Is close at hand;
So he's now after
Each and every man;
For he cannot match
Almighty God in a fight;
So he's after every man
With all his might.

The Devil's working overtime
To try to stop the Church Of God
From unifying its efforts to
Raise up an army that will trod
This world in power

And in might
Spreading the Gospel
With great light
To all who'll hear
With their heart,
Heed God's Word;
Then depart
From ways of sin,
And ways of shame,
And win the victory
Through Jesus Name.
The outcome of
This war we're in
Has been determined
Way back when
God began to create
A world with which
To relate.

P's

People Called Christians

Many people are called Christians;
But just a few actually know Christ,
And have the fruit to prove it
Dangling from their life.
Some people are Christian
Just merely in name;
While others are Christian
For monetary gain.
There are those that are Christian
Strictly just for fame;
While others are Christian
To hide their guilt and shame.
Those that know Christ
Spend time each day in prayer,
While searching His Word daily
To find anointing there;

So that they might become like Him
Allowing Him to be
The center and circumference
Of a life that's been set free.
But if you want to make it,
There is a key to know.
Those that actually make it
Will be those that Christ knows.

People Who

People who love darkness
Complain when they see the light.
People who love their sin
Are offended by those in the right.
People who use God's name in vain
Complain when others use it for good.
People who live for selfish gain
Find it hard to give themselves for another's good.
People who are stubborn in their ways
Find it hard to let others rule.
People who are of a rebellious nature
Look at authority as uncool.
People who love the light
Want to expel the darkness.
People who hate sin
Are drawn to righteousness.

People who understand how to use God's name
Use it for the glory of God.
People who live for others do
To express their love for God.
People who live in surrender
To the authority of Jesus Christ
Find it easy to submit
To Godly men throughout their life.

Perceptions

Many things can
Be viewed as sin
When viewed from
A certain perspective;
But carnal eyes
Can see no wrong,
As long as the flesh
Is on the throne.

✫ ✫ ✫

Playing Games?

If games with God
You must then play;
You must play well,
Prepared to say
The reasons for
The games you play;
Else you'll find yourself
In a bit dismay.

★ ★ ★

Plight Of The Accused

Once his good was evil spoken of
And compromise became his plight
He found it real hard
To come completely into the light.
Although peace of mind was what he wanted,
Healing was what he needed,
And spiritual insight was what he had,
But none of these could plant the seed
That would have cleansed his soul from sin
Or delivered his mind from guilt.
Condemnation had become his friend,
And his convictions seemed to just wilt.
Before he had known what he had done
He found that iniquity to him
Had really become fun;
And he found himself rejoicing
In the midst of this lie;

Which made the truth appear
As if it would make him fry;
For the only way that truth
Could really have set this man free
Would have been if he was willing
To walk completely into the light
So that all could then see.

Poetic Inspiration

Inspiration to the poet
Is like the wind.
The way he recognizes its presence
Is by feeling its gentle breeze;
Then listening for its sound;
Then, if the poet is successful,
The reader will catch
The wind of this inspiration
In his sail;
And will be carried along
The sea of its understanding
To the destination of encouragement

★ ★ ★

Poetic Justice

Will my body
Have to die,
And be planted
In the earth
Before I can see
The fruit of this,
My life and my work.
Most of the great poets
Of the past
Died before they received
The honor they so richly deserved.
God, that doesn't have to be;
Or does it?
Couldn't there be
One poet that acclaims greatness
Within his life time?
And couldn't that poet be me?
Not to elevate the talent;
But to bring all the glory to Thee?

Poets Of The Bible

This statement was once made,
"Poetry is not
A viable means
To communicate God's Word
To Sunday School Children."
And, Oh how
I wanted to tell him,
"Well, then you'd better
Cut out the Psalms.
Oh yes,
And the Proverbs as well.
By the way,
Job just happens to be
One long poem.
Also Ecclesiastes and
The Song of Solomon
Are poetic verse.
Oh yea,
Let's not sing in Sunday School either,
For someone will not understand the lyrics.
Throw out the song of Moses,
And Gideon's march,

Peter's mention of David in Acts 2;
As well as the rest of Peter's Sermon,
Because he quoted from Joel's poem.
In fact, if you take a closer look at the Bible,
You'll find that the Bible itself
Is just one Gigantic poem.
You see,
God chose to use men
That had Poetic talent
To pen His Word;
Because the very nature of prose
Is multiple application.
Just because we don't call them poets;
But chose to call them
Apostles, Prophets, Judges, etc . . . ;
Doesn't make them any less poets.

Prioritized

I don't ever want to Come to
Church Looking forward
To meeting someone
More than
Meeting with You, Lord,

I don't ever want to
Come to Church
Looking forward
To doing something
More than
Worshiping You, Lord,

I want my desires
To be prioritized
With my desires for You
As number one.

I never want
My desire for You
To ever fall below
Anything else
In my life
Or be in tow.

Practice Makes Perfect

"One of his disciples said unto him, Lord, teach us to pray, as John also taught his disciples" Luke 11:1

One can know how to handle and operate the most sophisticated of weapons; but it is not the one that knows how, but the one who takes action that wins the victory. It is a much more valuable lesson to learn to pray than it is to be taught all the intricacies of how to pray; for invariably it is the one that consistently and faithfully prays that becomes proficient at it. One can learn all the right words to say, the proper motivations to have, and even attain unto the wisdom of the right timing; but unless one actually prays, all of his wisdom and knowledge of prayer becomes vanity to him.

Prisoners Of Time

While encapsulated in a capsule of responsibilities that dictate the responses that can be made; will you go in or out, up or down, right or wrong? There is no in-between. Each decision has eternal ramifications. Each decision affects the lives of countless thousands that follow through this capsule called time. Time is a ruthless warden that holds us prisoner within his defining walls. He stops for no man. His only governor is God's eternal truth. He challenges every man, and yet is challenged by no man. Man, outside of God's Divinely ordained plan, is no match for time. Time holds us captive until the day of our eternal release by the judge of the quick and dead, the Lord Jesus Christ. At that point, we will pass through the great barrier into eternity; and only then will we know how many we have hurt and how many we have helped while traveling through this capsule called time. Right now I am, you are, we all are prisoners of time. Time is continually escaping us; but we will only escape time by our Divine appointment with eternity. The appointed time of our departure is set. And only the governor of time can change that date. What shall we do with time? Or even yet, What will time do with us? Will it age us, starve us, weaken us, or strengthen us? Will it love us, hate us, mold us or shape us? Will it help us, hurt us, strip us, or skirt us? Just what will it do with us while we are still prisoners of time?

Pure Obedience

Pure heart-felt obedience
To God's Living Word
Does not ever expect to
By the crowd be heard.
It doesn't seek after
Mere human acceptance,
Only for Divine favor
When it comes to reverence.
Pure obedience
Seeks not its own
As far as selfishness is concerned;
But the welfare of others
Is what it's looking to earn.
Obedience from
A pure heart of faith
And trust in God's Word
Is not tainted by ambition;
By greed it is not stirred.

Pure obedience
Is what we should desire;
For it will keep us from
The eternal fire
That'll be there
On the final stage
Along with Heaven
At the end of all ages.

2's

Quicken Me

Quicken my eyes to see
What you would have me to.
Quicken my ears to hear
Your Word which is so true.
Quicken my mouth to say
What you would have me to say.
Quicken my heart, oh Lord,
In every way.

Quicken my feet to walk,
Oh Lord, in your steps.
Quicken my faith so that,
Oh Lord, it is felt.
Quicken my mind to think
All the right thoughts.
Quicken my heart to know,
Oh Lord, that it's bought.

R's

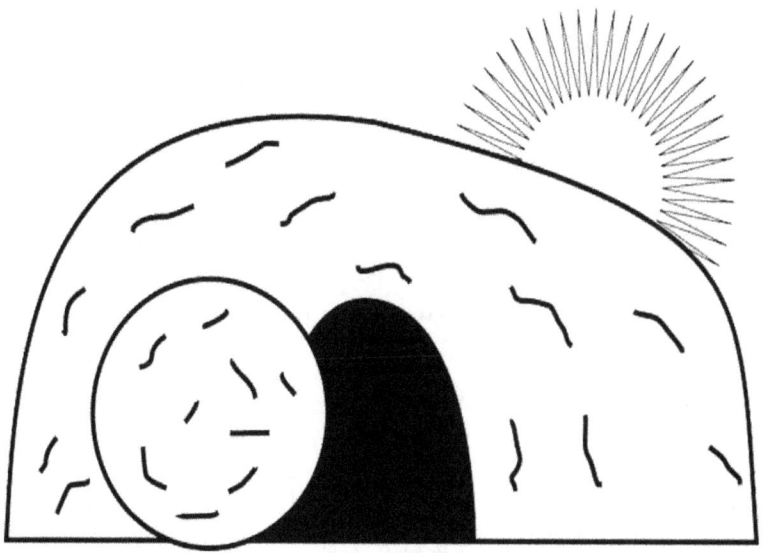

Real Beauty

What turns beauty into ugliness
Comes from deep within
When the heart is full of pride
And the lusts for sin.

What turns ugliness into beauty
Also finds its source within,
A broken and contrite heart
In repentance from all sin.

If the outer man is found
To be quite unattractive,
And the heart is broken
With a contrite spirit,
Then though the flesh is ugly
And hard to look upon,
There is a glow that's radiant
Coming from the inner spirit.

True beauty finds its source
In the heart that's full of grace,
Not polluted by vested interests
For popularity or place.

Yes, in a heart that is pure,
Not cluttered up with gilt
Over some shameful act
That keeps the mind in tilt.

Reasonable Lifestyle

What is your reason
For this lifestyle
That you live?
Is it just the season,
Or the way
That you give?
Why do you think you're right?
What is the basis of your stand?
Is it based upon God's light;
Or the words of common man?
Is this the way
You're gonna be;
Or will you change
Just because of me?
Oh, if you'll change
Just because of me;
You're not really standing at all.
My friend, You're not free.
You're really bound
By other's opinions.
That is what dictates
All of your decisions.

So be sure
That you're standing
In a solid place;
And that you're not shaken
'Til you're out of the race.
Stand firm and secure
Upon solid ground;
Then you'll be free;
And no longer bound.

Reasons Or Excuses

One and one is two.
Two and two is four.
Give me enough reasons
And I'll walk through that door.

Three and three is six.
Six and six is twelve.
Sometimes you make excuses
To put something on the shelf.

There are times;
And there are seasons.
There are excuses;
And there are reasons.

Though you may not understand
Why I'm sitting out;
I must assure you
That by God's grace
I'll make it
Beyond a shadow of a doubt.

Reasons

To serve the Holy
God above
In faithful
Undying love.
To live a life
Of holiness;
One that will please
The Prince of Peace.
These are reasons
To travel down
The righteous path
Of Christ the Lamb.

To shine a light
Into this world,
Revealing truth
The way unfurled.
To help a soul
To find this way,
And be there for
This soul to pray.
These are reasons

To travel down
The righteous path
Of Christ the Lamb.

To live a life
That shines so bright
That souls will see
How they can fight
To grab a hold
Of faith and truth,
Not just for themselves,
But for their youth.
These are reasons
To travel down
The righteous path
Of Christ the Lamb.

To impart this light
Into some dark soul
In hopes that they
Will become whole.
To teach a soul
The way back home,
To help that soul
Know he's not alone.
These are reasons
To travel down
The righteous path
Of Christ the Lamb.

To watch a child
Come into faith,
And enter into
His life course race.
To see his face
As he receives
True Living Water
As he believes.
All of these are reasons
To travel down
The righteous path
Of Christ the Lamb.

Recognize Your Blessings

Open up your eyes;
For there is something
That God wants you to see;
How beautiful that life is
Once He has set you free.
His blessings clearly show us
How much He really cares;
And when we're in His will
His blessings are always there.
Sometimes we fail to recognize
The blessings that God sends;
Because of our own selfishness
We cannot understand
That sometimes His blessing to us
Has others in mind;
And so our own benefit
Is what we cannot find.

But when you stop and look
At how God gets you to reach out;
And you start in others to believe,
And trust, and not doubt,
Then you might be able to see
That participating in life
Is the greatest blessing for thee.

Repentance

"R" is for the RESISTANCE
That you feel within your soul.
"E" is for that in ETERNITY
You'll want to be fully whole.
"P" is for your PRIDE
That you must put to death.
"E" is for the ENCOURAGEMENT
Of God's Spirit to pass this test.
"N" is for the NEW LIFE
That this prepares you for.
"T" is for when you TRUST GOD
You'll begin to win this war.
"A" is for the AUTHORITY
In Christ you will receive.
"N" is for that you'd NEVER
Thought you could believe.

"C" is for the Commitment
To Christ that you must make.
"E" is for that Each Time this happens to you
You're that much less a fake.

Revival Fires

Revival fires,
Start with me.
Help me burn out
All the chaff
As God's Spirit
Begins to expose
All sorts of carnal
Riff-raff.

As I seek To kill my flesh;
By sacrificing
What it wants;
Revival fires
Burn through me;
Leave nothing left
To haunt.

Revival fires,
Help me find
God's anointing
And His Power
That will change

My life completely
Starting this very hour.

Revival fires,
Where's the spark
That will ignite inside of me
A Holy, Godly fire so bright;
That it will draw
All those around
To come and watch me
Burn tonight.

Revival fires,
Start with me;
For as I give
All of me
Willing to burn with
Eternal flame;
I invite the Lord of Host
To send His Holy Rain;
Not to put out
This Holy Ghost Fire;

But to feed this hunger
And enhance this desire
To seek after God
With all that's within
To secure a relationship
With my Eternal Friend.

Righteousness, True Or False

Where true righteousness will always leave the door open to the dealings of God, self righteousness can actually become a barricade against any attempt of God to deal with the human soul. True righteousness can only be worked in the life that is faithfully following the leadership of the Holy Ghost through the Spirit-led application of God's Word. Self righteousness is worked by adhering to standards of apparel and/or conduct IN ORDER TO BE ACCEPTED by the status quo of a local church. For this reason peer pressure will almost automatically produce self righteous proselytes. It takes Holy Ghost conviction to produce true righteous behavior. This, by no means, negates the necessity of modest standards of apparel and/or conduct; but just merely explains the difference between the methods in which one comes to adhere to these standards; as well as the danger of failing to wait on God's dealing in an individual's life before introducing that soul to the concept of standards. When a soul is manipulated into putting on a set of standards through some form of peer pressure instead of waiting on Holy Ghost conviction, then the true dealing of God is by-passed; and that soul loses out on an element of divine blessings in his relationship with God. That same soul will eventually begin to resent the very standards he holds because of the absence of

430

these blessings. And when he perceives others receiving blessing after blessing who have not yet conformed to these standards, jealousy and envy will begin to spring up in his heart; and that soul will be prone to become a wolf in sheep's clothing intent on devouring unknowing souls. But when through Holy Ghost conviction a soul is led into keeping a particular set of standards, he is then given the opportunity to experience those blessings first hand, and is content to wait on God when it comes to someone else who has not yet conformed. This self righteous behavior (the jealous devouring of unknowing souls) was the plight of the Pharisee and Sadducee of Jesus' day; and is the reason why Jesus upbraided them often. They "WOULD IN NO WISE ENTER IN" and prevented "OTHERS" also. It is no wonder that the word says "ALL OUR RIGHTEIOUSNESS IS AS FILTHY RAGS." We must remind ourselves that God is the one who will raise up the standard in an individual's life, then confirm that standard through God-called Pastors. The will of God for any individual is as delicate as the unfolding of a flower. If you or I try to peel back its pedals, it will just crumble before us causing irreparable damage to the soul. But if we allow the Holy Ghost the opportunity to work, we will all be able to enjoy the beauty and blessing that God unfolds right before our eyes. And true righteousness will just unfold in our own individual lives as we strive to be faithful to dealings of the Holy Ghost.

S's

Saved By The Rain

Although many died
In that famous flood
That covered the whole earth
Including those that misunderstood
The seriousness of the promise
Of the coming rain
Until the very day
That the flood came.

Noah caught the drift
Of what the Master meant,
And built an Ark of gopher wood
That only God could sink.
The eight souls inside
Who had endured much pain
Had escaped the destruction;
For they were saved by the rain.

Elijah had spoke the word
That had shut up Heaven's door,
And brought about a drought
That made life a real chore.

For three long years, not a drop
Of water from Heaven came;
But when Elijah spoke again,
He was saved by the rain.

The Disciples gathered there
In that upper room
Waiting for the promise of God
That would come so very soon.
They received such awesome power
When that promise came;
For they were all delivered
And saved by the rain.

So, if you're in the bondage
Of sin's habits, desires, or fame,
And you want to be set free
From your guilt and shame,
You can receive God's power
As you seek to gain
The promise of the Holy Ghost,
And be saved by the rain.

Seeds Of Eternity

Once you have visited the Realm Of The Eternal, the realm of time seems to lose its appeal. Once you have realized the value of just the concept of Eternal Life, material things begin to lose their ability to entice you. But unless you cultivate these Seeds Of Eternity, it is not long before you begin to reevaluate them according to the analytical philosophies of the human existence. The only thing you can never deny is the fulfillment that you felt standing in the Realm Of The Eternal Spirit of God, that feeling that you never wanted to leave His Holy Presence, that desire to do whatever it takes to secure an everlasting relationship with Jesus Christ that would catapult you into Eternity with Him. Just how much is it worth to you to spend forever with the Creator Of All Things, the Eternal One that is the very basis of all that True Love is? What scales do you use to measure an Everlasting Relationship With An All Powerful, All Knowing, Ever Existing God? How can it even be compared to this temporary limited existence we all know in this material world? Just the authority alone that believers obtain is invaluable; that ability to speak to situations and see them reversed right before your eyes; that ability to see beyond the appearance of things and understand the underlying motives of the hearts of people involved in

435

particular circumstances. How can a price tag be too large to pay for such a gift? When you lay time right next to Eternity, just how do they compare? Is not time just a tiny spec and Eternity a continuous straight line with no beginning or end? Is not life without Jesus Christ the essence of all loneliness as well as the apideme of chaos and confusion? God is a God Of Order And Dominion; and contained within His Domain is real peace, and within His Order is true safety. Submission to His Plan brings real contentment and cleansing. So why stay outside? Come on in. Yes, come on into the Presence Of The Eternal One where the light of His Existence will begin exposing the hidden attitudes of your heart in order to allow His Blood to cleanse your soul. Allow Him to walk the corridors of your heart, knocking on all the closed doors. And when He does knock, open them up unto Him so He can sup with you in Holy Communion. A Communion that is more than just a piece of bread and a cup of juice or wine; but This Communion is actually your participation in a relationship with an Eternal God. The eating of the bread and the drinking of the cup merely signifies that relationship and reaffirms our covenant vows. The reality of that Communion is found in the Spirit, That Realm Of The Eternal, that place of actual At/one/ment where our spirit becomes one with His Spirit, where our mind becomes one with His Mind, where our emotions mingle with His Emotions, where our will joins forces with His Will, and where our bodies become animated by the sheer joy of being completely engrossed in His Majesty. Once we find this type of Communion we will never want to let go of it; but, to the *contrary, we will want to cultivate it often, pulling out all the weeds and grasses that would hinder the growth of such a relationship. Don't you want this type of relationship with the Lover Of Your Soul? He desires that with you. That's why He invites you right now to come on into His Holy Presence and experience what True Communion really is.*

Seeds

Seeds,
Before they grow,
Begin so small;
Just a thought or a word,
Or maybe a Divine call;
But once it's conceived
And begins to sprout,
Doesn't take it very long
To just burst out;
Pushing aside the shell
That once hindered life;
Pushing upward and upward
And finally into light.
Then as it begins to grow tall,
Deeper the roots will grow
Reaching down into the soil
To find a life-giving flow.
Soon it begins to mature;
Then to multiply
By producing more seeds
Before it then must die.

Self Pity's Eyes

There is only one thing clear
In the eyes of self pity;
And it's that we are near
The end of our misery;
For nothing could be worse
Than what we're now going through;
Then when worse does come along
We really don't know what to do;
For self pity only looks
To that which is within;
And it cannot see what's
Outside of its pen.
But if only we could just
Peer out of this jail;
Then surely we could see
A glimpse of a trail;
That if we should walk
Down this dimly lit path,
We'll find a way out
Of self pity's wrath.
Then the farther we'd walk
The brighter will be

The path that'll lead us
To our victory.
If you think you can make it
With your eyes on yourself;
You are sadly mistaken
And losing your health;
For the path that leads out
Of self pity's grasp
Is looking on others
Whose needs you can clasp.

Show Me, Lord

I wish that I
Could pin point
Just what You're
Trying to say.
I know You're trying
To speak to me;
And so I'll just
Watch and pray.
I feel Your presence lingering near,
And knocking on my heart's door.
So, here I am, oh Lord.
Come and sup with me some more.
Help me to hear and understand
With an open heart;
And respond to Your presence
Right from the very start.
What must I do, oh Lord,
To stay within Your Grace;
To stay within Your favor
Traveling at Your pace?
I want only to move forward;
Not to stop, or fall back.

I want my life to please You;
So, help me stay on track.
Speak to me, dear Jesus.
Give me wisdom from above;
So, I can continue to serve you
From a heart that's filled with love.
I'm not trying to please a man
Unless it takes it to please You;
For Your favor is what I long for.
Help me keep a heart that's true.

Shut Up Flesh

Sometimes it's hard
To shut the mouth of the flesh;
That cries day and night
For you to satisfy its wish.
But when you are determined
To put this voice to death;
And wrestle it down;
You will find peace and rest.
For with fasts and with prayer
You fight your flesh to win;
And after this kind of struggle
The victory you will win.
But fasts alone
Cannot conquer this foe.

It takes the prayer of faith
To deliver blow after blow;
'Til quiet and submissive
The flesh will follow behind
The leading of God's Spirit
And the Christian mind.

Signals

As we drive to and fro
On the highways of life,
We find the roads are filled
With all sorts of signal lights.
These lights tell us when to stop,
And when to go on ahead,
When to be careful as we go,
Or when to look for the red;
When it's okay to just turn right;
Or stay in the traffic and just fight.
As long as we carefully obey
What each signal directs
We should have a very peaceful ride
Unless some other driver neglects,
And veers right over
Into our path,
Only to incur a reluctant fit
Of our unintentional wrath.

Though signals can be annoying at times,
They are necessary to life;
For without them life would be so chaotic,
And filled with all sorts of strife.

Sin May Be Fun

Your sin may be fun;
But your fun won't last;
For your fun will be destroyed
By the guilt of your past.

☆ ☆ ☆

Sister Maureen

"M" is for how MIGHTY
She becomes in prayer.

"A" 'is for the AUTHORITY
She has when she is there.

"U" is for the UNDERSTANDING
Nature of her ways.

"R" is for how RESPONSIVE
That she is when she prays.

"E" is for the ETERNAL VALUES
That she holds.

"E" is for EACH BURDEN
She takes to God so bold.

"*N*" *is for the NEW LIFE*
That she has found in prayer.

And her name is sister MAUREEN
Whose heart is filled with care.

Some Angels

Some angels have fallen;
Others stand their post,
Carefully attending
To the Holy Ghost.
Some angels are for battle;
Some are there to aid,
Whenever we are helpless,
And cannot make the grade.
Some angels are for good times;
Some are for the bad;
Some for when we're happy;
Some for when we're sad.
Some angels are there to nurse us
From sickness back to health.
Some are there to help us
From poverty back to wealth.
Some are there to hold us,
And keep us in the way.
Some are there to mold us
As we seek the Lord and pray.
Some are there to lead us,
And gently take our hand,

Taking us step by step
Out of a foreign land.
But all in all God's angels
Are there for me and you
To help us along the way
To walk a path that's true.

Some Folks

Some folks walk
To the left;
While others walk
To the right.

Some folks walk
In the dark;
While others walk
In the light.

Some folks carry
Their burdens;
While others give
Their's away,

By taking them to
The foot of the Cross
Each time they kneel
Down to pray.

Some folks hold
Everything in;
While others let

Everything out.

Some folks live
By faith;
While others live
By doubt.

Some folks believe
In God's mercy;
While others
In Justice Divine;

And live out their lives
In the constant fear
They'll never connect
Up to the Vine.

Some folks hold
Grudges forever;
While others
Forgive right away.

Some folks never
Release love;
While others share
Their's day by day.

Some People Fight

Some people fight
With the fist clinched hand
Using weapons that were made
With the hands of man.

Some people fight
With the sharp cutting word
That wounds the inner spirit
When their message is heard.

Some people fight
Through prayer with God's Word
Bringing thoughts into captivity
By submitting to the Lord.

Though each will find some victory
Through the method they find,
Only one will truly last,
'Til the end of time.

Sometimes

It sometimes takes a storm
To bring a much needed rain.
Sometimes healing can
Only come through pain.
Times must sometimes get harder
Before they can get better.
And sometimes it must get darker
Before it can become lighter.

So if you see a storm
Coming upon your horizon,
You can believe for the rain.
And if you know that
Healing's on its way,
You can endure the pain.

And if you can see that
Better times are just right ahead,
You can endure the hardness.
And if you know that
The Sun's going to soon bring the light,
You can endure the darkness.

Sometimes I Wonder

Sometimes I wonder
If I'll survive
Long enough
To see the Christ
Coming in
The sky for us
And see the Church
With Him go up.

Sometimes I wonder
If I'll be here
When the Anti-Christ
Rules in fear
As Satan's wrath
Is then unleashed
Against the Jews
Destroying peace.

Oh Lord,
Prepare me now,
So I can know
From You just how
To be ready
To go up
And be with You
In that great sup.

Sometimes One Needs

Sometimes one needs to
Take his own advise,
Cry out to God
Without any spice,
Being totally honest
And pure in heart,
Letting God be the one
To create the spark.

Sometimes one needs to
Stand up and fight,
Cry out to God
With all his might
Completely humble,
And yet lion bold,
Making absolutely certain
To God his need is told.

Sometimes one needs to
Straighten up his act,
Call out on God,
And then make a pact
That he'll turn and do
Just the right thing;
Then when he's done,
God's glory sing.

Sometimes You Just Cannot Explain

Sometimes you just cannot explain
What God does now and again.

When God does
What only He can do,
That is what to man
Is just impossible,
You just cannot explain
With a natural word
What to most of us
Is virtually unheard.

When God speaks
In a way that only He can,
To get His children
To understand,
You just cannot explain
With a natural word
What to most of us
Has virtually not heard.

No, sometimes you just cannot explain
How God meets our need now and again;
For He is God, and we are but men.
When it is beyond our ability,
It is got to be Him.

Spiritual Warfare

"S" is for your "SACRIFICE"
Through which you enter this fight.

"P" is for the "POWER OF GOD"
That becomes your might.

"I" is for the "INSPIRATION"
Received through the Word and prayer.

"R" is for the "REALITY"
Of this Spiritual Warfare.

"I" is for the "INCREDIBLE POWER"
Of Gods Holy Living Word.

"T" is for the "TRUTH"
That becomes your mighty sword.

"U" is for His "UNDENIABLE"
Presence that you feel.

"A" is for the "AUTHORITY OF GOD",
Your rightful place with zeal.

"L" is for the "Love" of God
That motivates your fight.

"W" is for the "Winning"
That you expect to do tonight.

"A" is for your "Abiding In Him";
For this will make you whole.

"R" is for the "Resistance"
Of the enemies of your soul.

"F" is for the "Faith"
That will give you strength tonight.

"A" is for how "Acceptable"
Is your good and faithful fight.

"R" is for your "Righteous Duty"
Which it is to answer Gods Call.

"E" is for "Eternity"
The reason for it all.

Standards

A standard is a wall
Built up to protect
Whatever is contained within it
From any external effects.
It is established to keep out
The external influences
Of both fear and doubt.
But oft' times it keeps
All bound up within
The testimony of faith
Meant to conquer sin;
For when the standard is kept
Out of fear instead of faith,
It actually keeps
The light from being seen
And the soul from grace.

So, when you raise a standard
To then protect your soul,
Be sure it's kept in faith,
Making conviction your goal.
Make sure you please the Lord,
Not seeking the praise of men,
So that your life
Can be transparent
Allowing the light to be seen.

Strongholds

There are many strongholds,
Of which some do stand out;
Like the addiction to smoking,
The drink, or to being all drugged out.
But there are some strongholds
That are not quite as plain;
Like that of prejudice,
Pride, guilt, or shame.
The stronghold of a grudge
Due to offenses unforgiven
Opens the door for hatred
Of whom that one's resenting.
Strongholds are merely doorways
That allow manipulation
By demonic forces'
Attempts at intervention.

So, if one allows a stronghold
To exist within his life,
He should not be at all surprised
When he endures consistent strife.

Sunday Morning

Sunday morning;
Time to pray,
And worship God
All of this day;
For it's set aside
To give to Him
That which actually
Belongs to Him.
"Seek ye first
The Kingdom of God."
The first day of the week
To church I trod
To pour out my soul
In worship and prayer;
For I know that Jesus
Will meet me there.

Sunday morning
Is dedicated to
Giving You Lord
What belongs to You;
All my affection
In worship and praise;
And taking this time
Your Name to raise.

Sunday School

Sunday school,
Children coming,
Expecting to receive
A little something
To help them through
This life down here,
And perhaps
A little cheer;
To teach them all
About God and life;
To show them how
To cope with strife;
To help them pray
For answers needed;

And show them when
Words should be heeded;
But all in all,
So they will know
The Savior's will
Is the way to go.

T's

"Take Out The Garbage"

"There is a time and a season for every purpose under Heaven" as the writer of the book of Ecclesiastes puts it. One day the Lord spoke to me, "It is time for you to tAke out the GArBAGe." I had just arrived at the Sunday School room on Bake Sale Sunday morning when I noticed that the garbage had not been removed from the previous Sunday. So, I grabbed the garbage bag and began walking down to the dumpster when I heard that still small voice speaking to me, "It is time for you to tAke out the GArBAGe." And I knew with an inner awareness that God was speaking of more than the physical garbage I was carrying. But He was speaking of inner attitudes that attach themselves to our spirit from day to day. Before too long, just like the kitchen or bedroom at home, our lives become cluttered with all sorts of spiritual garbage; carnal baggage that weights us down and hinders us from doing His will in our lives. So when that voice told me to "tAke out the GArBAGe," I quickly knew it was time to do *some spiritual cleanup. A time of introspection was needed to find those things that were cluttering my mind and spirit that were hindering my focus on God's will for my life, to find those little distractions that were drawing my attention to the petty things in my life.*

Takes A Decision

It takes a DECISION
To have COURAGE;
And yet it takes COURAGE
To make a DECISION.
It takes DISCIPLINE
To make a COMMITMENT;
And yet it takes a COMMITMENT
To maintain DISCIPLINE.
It takes DETERMINATION
To build CHARACTER;
And yet it takes CHARACTER
To be DETERMINED
To carry a project
All the way to completion.

Thanks For Everything

Thank you, Lord
For everything
You have done for me.
Thank you for coming
Into my life
To set me free
To worship and
To give you praise
All the rest
Of my days.
Thank you, Lord
For everything
You have done for me.

Thank you, Lord
For everything
You have done for me.
Thank you for coming
Into my life
To set me free
To worship and
To praise your name,

You who are
Always the same.
Thank you, Lord
For everything
You have done for me.

Thanksgiving

"T" is for the TIMES
That God has seen us through.

"H" is for HOW OFTEN
He has strengthened me and you.

"A" is for the ANGELS that
Are watching our every step.

"N" is for that NO ONE
Can do without His help.

"K" is for His KINDNESS
He displays daily toward us.

"S" is for the SUFFERING
Of the savior Christ Jesus.

"G" is for the GIFT
Of that precious Holy Ghost.

"I" is for the INCREDIBLE WAY
That He provides for this great earthly host.

"V" is for the Victory
That He bought for us to share.

"I" is for the Inspiration
Of His Word which shows us He cares.

"N" is for that Never
Will He leave us alone.

"G" is for that I'm Grateful
For all that God has done.

That Dusty Old Book

No one really knows the wealth
That's in that dusty old book on the shelf.

Men search for riches,
And then for fame;
And go through so
Very much pain;
Not really knowing
Of the great wealth
That's in that dusty old book on the shelf.

Men hunt for treasures
The whole world o'er,
Traveling from this,
And to that shore;

Not really knowing
Of the great wealth
That's in that dusty old book on the shelf.

No one really knows the wealth
That's in that dusty old book on the shelf.

That Ole Wolf Spirit

That ole wolf spirit
Usually hungers
For all of the wrong things;
Attention and power;
That selfish ambition
Doesn't care just who it stings.
It manipulates, growls at,
And even steps on those
That dare to get in its way;
But you'll be amazed
Just who it is
Because they pretend to pray.
They look so alive
And put on a show
That'll fool the carnal eye;
But if you're discerning
And know God's Word
You'll see through their sheepish disguise.
Sometimes wolves may
Run in a pack
To gang up upon a soul;
Especially a poor

Defenseless lamb
Not yet grounded in the Word.
That's why God
Has called out Shepherds
To protect and feed His flock.

God helps them see
That ole wolf spirit
To put an end to his plot.

That Void Within

Life is so busy
In its times and seasons,
And sometimes abrupt
For seemingly no reason.
Sometimes life
Allows you to progress;
But so many times it will
Just cause you to regress;
And though you may want
To quickly proceed;
You may have to just wait
While God meets your need.
You may think
That what you actually need is
To be surrounded with friends,
Your life then to bless;
But it could be that
What you really need is Him;
And 'til you come to know this,
Loneliness you befriend.

So, open up your heart,
And let His word in.
It will be a light
That'll reveal doubt and sin;
And show you the way
To fill that void within.

The Analytical Mind

"How much can I afford
To give to the Lord?"
That is the question
That we would find
Buried deep within
The analytical mind;
Calculating the investment
By the expected return,
Not truly comprehending the scales,
Nor how hot Hell's fire will burn.
The analytical mind
Not only counts the cost,
But it watches everyday
To be sure that nothing's lost.

The Battered Woman

This is about a woman who is the victim
Of an abusive husband. Her only hope
Is her own fear; but her own love pushes her fear aside.

Though battered and torn,
She won't look forlorn;
For she loves the man
That has done
To her this wrong.
Though it's to her loss,
She'll carry this cross;
For she loves the one
To whom she's paid this cost.
She covers it all
Behind this great wall
That her love drives her
To build up so tall.
No one will know;
For she won't let it show,
Though she's beaten at home,
Blow after blow.
This woman, you see,

She's nameless to me,
Though each day
One of her faces I see.
I'll never know;
For she won't let it show;
This pain that she feels
She has come to know.
So I will pray
For this woman today,
That she'll be delivered,
Somehow and someway.

The Battle At Its Thickest

When demonic forces surround us
And bombard us day and night
We face temptation to give in
And give up this daily fight.

When the battle's at its thickest
This fight against the flesh
Is when we need the Lord
To give us peace and rest.

God has promised us the victory
If only we can trust
That He will intervene
For His will is a must

But if we continue fighting
In the strength that is our own
We will eventually be entrapped
By one of Satan's clones.

So, do not trust so heavily
Upon your own will to fight this foe
But lean upon the Lord Jesus
And His Grace to just say, "NO".

The Bible

The Bible is a book,
Unlike any other book,
That speaks of life and God,
And so much that's overlooked.
When one meditates
Upon its pages
With an open heart,
Its message will reveal
A new place one can start
To live life to its fullest
With an eternal goal
To make one's way to Heaven
Saved and completely whole.
When one memorizes
Its message,
It then becomes a guide
To direct one through life's trials
Delivering one safely to the other side.

When one abides
Within its words,
And those words abide in him,
It creates such faith and hope
One cannot help but win.

The Blood Of Jesus Christ

The Blood of Jesus Christ
Is powerful indeed.
It took that precious blood
To meet man's deepest need.
It cleanses the sin sick soul,
And washes the stain of sin,
Heals the broken man,
Making him whole again.
Its given as a token,
A sign so spirits know,
This soul belongs to Jesus,
And is never to be sold.
It serves as our protection
From the angel of death,
To stand between our soul
And God's awesome wrath.

Its also a part of mercy
That this blood is available to us;
For not one ounce of this great blood
Does any of us deserve.

★ ★ ★

The Bonds Of Liberty

People that deal
With intense loneliness
Have the privilege
To explore the depths
Of the sea
Of emotional anxiety;
For when they see
The sights of this land
And the chains
That hold them at bay;
Then once they are
Finally set free,
They can truly appreciate
The bonds of liberty.

Now, if one thinks
That freedom has no bonds,
They are merely deceived
And don't really understand
What it truly means
To be free.

★ ★ ★

The Call

There is a call going forth
Throughout this great land
For all God's people
To take a stand.
We've got to stand up;
And we've got to fight
For the good,
And for the right;
For if we fail
To take our stand,
We'll see the demise
Of the righteous man;
For the enemy's launching
His final campaign
To wage war on
The righteous man.

The call goes out
Across this land
For all God's people
To take a stand
Against the sin

And degradation
That's infected
This great nation.
We must stand up
And be counted;
For persecution on us
Will soon be mounted.
Our freedom to worship
Just as we please
Could easily be lost
lest we go to our knees,
And see if God
Would intervene,
And spare us from
What's now unseen.

The Dark Corner

There is one sin,
And then yet another;
So many times repented of,
And yet not fully covered;
For there is yet inside
This calloused heart of mine
An old dark and dreary corner
Where no light has shined.
One day, I know is coming
A revelation of His love
That'll flood this old dark corner,
And envelope it like a glove; '
Til revealed is the source
Of the snare of sin
On that day, I'll rejoice;
For that's when love will win.

Until then I'll repent,
And then repent again;
'Til the day that love will conquer,
'Til the day that love will win.

The Day Of Deliverance

The day of deliverance
Can really only come
Once all the battles are fought,
And all the victories are won.

But unless you take up the fight
You will never win;
And total defeat
Will be your final end.

Oh, but should you fight
Each and every battle hard,
The taste of victory
Can become your reward;

And once you've won the victory
O'er the last and final foe,
You'll walk in deliverance,
And be a slave no more.

The Defensive Mind

The defensive mind
Puts up a shield
To protect the heart
From pain or hurt;
But sometimes when
This shield is up
It keeps the heart
In a bitter murk.
When bitterness is
Growing there,
It becomes real hard
To truly care;
And the shield that keeps
The heart from pain
Also keeps in
This bitter stain.
Eventually the pain
That grows within
Becomes much greater
Than its external pen.
Sometimes one needs
To take a risk

Let down this wall,
Unclench the fist,
And allow someone
To penetrate,
So one then can
Actually escape
From within these walls
So as to find
Freedom from
The defensive mind.

The End Of Time

We really need to think about the end,
Yes, the end of time;
Or at least the end of life,
The end of our chance to shine.
We need to consider how short the days,
The few we have yet left,
To redeem each and every moment
Before they're victimized by theft.
Oh the enemy of our souls
So deceives us to distract
And keep us from the will of God,
God's plan for us to enact.
We must each find the righteous path
That God would have us to take;
So by the rapture of the church
Each one of us could then escape
The perilous times coming on this world
That all who's left will see;

And before it's over
Only few will recover
To escape and then find peace.
So let us all consider and think over
How to live our lives to shine
To lead many souls to a better place
Which can be found at the end of time.

The Finish Line

This man, though crippled
By arthritis pain,
Knew that he
Had much to gain;
So, with all his might
He did strain
To reach this Finish Line.

Though pain shot through
His joints so tight,
He still struggled
With all his might,
Knowing he'd lose
If he did not fight
To reach this Finish Line.

With stiffened up joints,
And determination of mind,
Careful consideration
The next step to find,
With grace of a very
Different kind
So, to reach this Finish Line.

Though no one else
Was in this race,
He still struggled
To Keep In pace,
Hoping to find
A little more grace
To reach this Finish Line.

And when he made
His final step,
Tears did flow
As this man wept;
For thanksgiving of heart
Is what he felt
When he reached this Finish Line.

For because this man
He did obey
What Christ the Lord
To him did say,
In answer to
What he did pray,
His healing he did find.

Though you may suffer
When you choose to do
What Christ the Lord
Has told you to,
A special grace
Awaits for you
As you reach your Finish Line.

The Fruit

Love is the fruit of acceptance.
Joy is the fruit of righteousness.
Peace is the fruit of discipline.
Long suffering is the fruit of hoping.
Gentleness is the fruit of consideration.
Goodness is the fruit of giving.
Faith is the fruit of believing.
Meekness is the fruit of receiving.
Temperance is the fruit of testing.

★ ★ ☆

The Gift Of Grace

The gift of grace
Moves within those
That have so they can give
To those in need,
Especially to those
Who cannot repay
With money, service,
Or any kind of deed
To bless the unfortunate
With clothes or with food
Or maybe just meet
A financial need.
This gift of grace
That moves within
Those that have to give
Is sent by God
To meet these needs
And make it easier
For them to live.

The Gods And Goddesses Of Hollywood And Toontown

The delusion is subtle, but nonetheless real; and most of modern man is falling for it hook, line, and sinker. Knowing that many elements of what is presented on the tube are usually fiction or at least changed from the facts for various reasons, we still take much of it as reality. We simply accept it as some sort of fictional reality even though it portrays how immoral and sinful man can be, not necessarily how he actually is. The picture that Hollywood presents makes it seem as though the sin factor within our cultures is an inescapable phenomenon and that righteous men are a rare commodity in this time in which we live. The public seems to be so deluded by this perspective of the world and the human race that trust is slowly becoming extinct, fear is ruling in the hearts and lives of humanity as a whole, and hope is becoming as slippery as a wet bar of soap for most of the people of the world. Now, those that present this delusion to humanity are held in the highest esteem and are placed high upon pedestals. In fact, some of them are fanatically honored and sometimes even worshiped. Most of them are emulated by us through our manner of dress, the way we carry ourselves, and sometimes

512

even in the way we talk. In our cultures, they have been somewhat deified by our societies as the gods and goddesses of this world. Hollywood calls them "Stars". Even animated characters have been elevated to a high standing and are even given seemingly immortal characteristics, for though they get run over, beaten to a pulp, or even blown up, they just keep right on going as if nothing had ever happened; thus creating in the mind of the viewer an illusion of deity. This illusion is being peddled daily to our children through various animated cartoon series. Is it any wonder that we have children today that cannot distinguish between fiction and reality, children that kill other children or even adults with the illusion that everything will continue as they were before no matter what they have done or will do. This is the idolatry of our present day, the worship of animated heroes or fictional characters in action films. The Stars of these productions have become the gods and goddesses of Hollywood and Toontown. Hollywood presents its main characters as invincible humanity, whether that main character is good or evil, moral or immoral, righteous or sinful; therefore, to the mind of the viewer, this main character is the "Star" (or god) of the show.

The Great Delusion

Sometimes past abuses
Can really distort our vision;
And create within us
This very strong delusion.
This delusion tries to tell us
That our God is actually mad;
And has determined for us
Only that which is bad;
But if we can just catch
A real glimpse of His mercy,
We'll begin to understand that
He really just wants to set us free.
Now once we are affected
By these delusive thoughts
We really cannot trust
The image they have wrought.
This version of God's image
That they paint for us
Is actually just a lie
That each of us must
Pull right down in prayer;
In doing so, we must fast

To receive a Holy Anointing
For the strength then to cast
Off this great delusion;
So we might then see
That the One True God
Has really set us free.

The Hand

I was going down
For the last time,
Completely disconnected
From the True Vine,
Trying everything
That I could find
To get a little
Peace of mind;
When all of the sudden
Out reached to me
A hand that seemed to come
From Eternity;
Reaching right on
Into our time
To help me to
The right way find;
And when I took
A hold of that hand,
It led me to a rock
On which I could stand.
Now I'm no longer
Sinking fast;

But standing firm and solid
Above my past;
So I give thanks to the one
That took my hand;
And led me to
My promised land.

The Hidden Word

What is it that keeps
A soul from sin
When it is tempted
Time and again?
What is it that keeps
A soul at bay
No matter what others
May do or say?
What is it that moves
One to forgive
When through other's faults
Pain and woe he lives?
It is the Word He's hidden away
Within his heart
From day to day.

The Hostess

Jody doesn't smile
While she walks down each isle;
And when you look
Into her eyes,
You can see right
Through her disguise.
You see, she's trying
To hide the pain;
For past relationships
Have caused her much strain;
And she's so afraid
To tell anyone.
And should they ask her,
She'll just run;
For all this strife's
In her private sphere;
This pain that keeps her
From being here.
Oh if she only knew
That God Almighty
Would help her through.
He's calling and calling;

Watching and waiting;
For Jody to come
With her heart just breaking.
He'd take the two parts
Of her broken heart;
And put them right
Back together again.
Yes, God wants for
Her broken heart to mend.
Oh, and He'll do more
Than mend her heart;
For He'll give to her
A brand new start;
Then show her how
To live again,
Free from pain,
And will be her friend.

The Hour Of Prayer

Twas the hour of prayer,
And no one was there,
And all because
They did not care.
What a horrible shame;
Because Jesus came,
And found the place empty
Again and again.
In His Word, you know,
He said He would show
Where in His name
We would gather;
To forsake us He said, "No."
His promise is there
For us to claim in prayer;
So, my friend,
Why weren't you there?

The Last Day Of Time

'Twas the Last day of time before eternity began,
And all around the world, life was still the same.
No one was repenting or living for Him;
Everyone was selfish and continuing to sin.
When all of the sudden came a giant blast,
The sound of a trumpet, Jesus coming at last.
He was riding a white horse and leading the way,
The Saints coming with Him all in bright array.
The armies were gathered and ready to fight;
But no match for the Master, who was shining the Light.
The mountain was split, that great Olivet,
When His feet came to rest, the battle was set.
He fought with The Sword that came from His mouth,
That brought judgment to all, East, West, North, and South.
As the battle continued over hill, valley, and plain;
The blood of men ran to the horses mane.
Then spake the Lord Jesus at the end of it all,

"It is finished,
The End of The Law."

The Letter

I know you would like to know Me, for the longing I see in your eyes reveals the hunger that is in your soul. But the busy-ness of your lifestyle is preventing you from seeking after Me the way that you would like to. You think that you are trapped in this lifestyle you are living in; but you just don't see that it is all in a choice. A simple decision on your part could turn your whole life around. And what appears to be major hindrances in your life would just vanish as if they never existed if you would only make up your mind to turn and seek after Me; for I am the Lover Of Your Soul, the All Existent One, the Almighty. And when you seek Me with your whole heart you will find Me; for every step you take towards Me, I will take ten towards you. For every word of praise you render unto Me will hasten My advances toward you; for I long to caress you with My Spirit. I long to hear your heart felt calling of My name; for you are the apple of My eye. I'm always pondering ways to get your attention. I search for ways to answer your prayers in hopes that you will notice. I stand at the gates of Heaven with My ear inclined towards you in the mere hope that your very next word could be your call; and I stand ready to answer you. So, come unto Me with your weariness and find rest. Come unto Me with your brokenness and find joy.

Come unto Me with your pain and find healing. Come unto Me with your emptiness and let Me fill it to the full with My Love. If you will turn and walk towards Me, I will run towards you; for I love you. I am your Creator, your Friend, your Counselor, your God.

All My Love,

JESUS CHRIST

The Light Of The World

Jesus, who is
The light of the world,
At Calvary,
His love was unfurled;
And right now
His grace is being shed,
And all because
On the Cross He bled;
And very soon
We'll see Him come again;
for we know that
It's part of His plan
To redeem a people
Called by His name.
Others, on that day
Will be ashamed.

The Lonely Side Of Christmas

Some people have never seen
The lonely side of Christmas;
That place that sorrow is in;
And the tears just won't pass.
As much happiness that
This holiday has brought;
Some have seen the lonely side
And the broken heart;
And all because
A loved one passed;
Or maybe just forgotten,
To send a card,
A gift which has
Some love inside begotten.
The lonely side of Christmas;
No one really wants to see it;
Until they find
That it's them
That they're seeing in it.
So when you're sitting home;
With family and with friends;
Enjoying opening presents;

And the fruit that giving brings;
Remember someone's hurting;
And in their hour of despair,
And at that very moment needs
For someone just to care.

The Master Procrastinator

The master procrastinator
Knows just how
To put off anything
To a time much better than now.

The master procrastinator
Knows just when
To put things off until;
For the now is not as good as the then.

And when the then has become the now,
And the now has become the then,
The master procrastinator
Just puts it off again.

The Melody, Rythem, And Message

Just as the melody line
Completes the song;
So does the right woman
Complete the man.
A single man is a song
Without a melody.
A single woman is a melody
In search of a song to complete.
The life of a couple
Bound together in marriage
Can be summed up in this way:
He is the rythem;
She is the melody;
And their covenant before
God Is the lyric or message
That either glorifies
Or denies their God.

The Mordecai Call

There's a call going out
To the (Mordecai)s of our land
To pray for the Spirit of Esther
To rise up and take a stand.
Oh Mordecai,
Please lay in the gate,
In dust and ashes
On the Lord God to wait;
For the spirit of Haman
Is at work in our land
Trying to destroy
God's people again.
It's time for a fast
By one and by all,
All of God's people,
Both the great and the small.
It's time for a prayer
From everyone's heart
To rise up unto God
Like one mighty shout,
"Lord, save your people
From this Haman-like plan,

And reveal to our leaders
The demise of this stand";
For the loss of our freedom
To worship our God
Is what we will reap
If we do not prod.
We must stand and fight
With shield and with sword,
Not in the carnal,
But through faith with the word.
The call must go out
For one mighty fast
By all of God's people
If victory will last.
This fast can't be limited
To a denomination or two;
But invite all who claim
To be faithful and true;
For when we join together
In one mind and accord,
God will work miracles
Through our faith in His word;
And we'll see a mighty work
In this nation of ours
When we're linked together

In faith and in power.
So establish the days
And publish them quick.
Call forth all God's people
To give the spirit of Haman a lick.
So the gallows he's building
For those who would pray
Will become his own snare
In that great day.

The Open Door

There is an open door
Right in front of you;
Waiting for your answer;
What are you going to do?

Will you just walk away
And ignore what's possible;
Or will you take a step of faith;
And that door just step on through?

Will you let the fear of failure
Keep you from potential success;
Or will you allow determination
Help you find what God will bless?

The Paradox

If I were a beggar
Begging for food,
Not to be heard
Would be to me rude.

If I were a rich man
Watching the tube,
The voice of the beggar
Would be to me rude.

This is a paradox
If you can believe,
Both men need each other
To fulfill their need.

The beggar needs the rich man,
Now that's easy to see,
And the rich man needs the beggar
If he wants to be free.

The beggar's eyes are open.
His need, he can see;
But blinded by his riches

The rich man only thinks he is free.

Bound up in emptiness
That riches can breed
When mingled with selfishness
It creates a great need.

But the only thing that
Can set this rich man free
Is to willingly reach out
And meet this beggar's need.

The Place

There is a place
We all will see.
A place where many
Will be set free.
Yet many there
Will be yet bound;
Those in whom sin
Is still yet found.

So, prepare yourself
Before you go;
For the times at hand,
Though no one really knows
The exact moment
That God will call
And say to his soul,
"That will be all".

At this place
That all will see,
Is where all men
Will bend the knee,
And confess the name
Of Jesus Christ the Lord;
While they receive
Their just reward.

The Power
That Lies In Reach

To stand between
A man and death;
To take command,
And conquer it;
To command the angel
In Jesus name;
To fight the invisible,
And conquer pain:

Oh the power
That lies in reach
When we heed God's word
As we hear one preach.

To speak the truth

That frees from sin;
To fight the battle
'Til the war you win;
To come to grips
With conviction's word;
'Til the heart is clean,
'Til His voice is heard:

Oh the power
That lies in reach
When we heed God's word
As we hear one preach.

To command in faith,
And see it done;
To walk so straight,
The victory's won;
To see God's power
Right before your eyes;
To watch demons flee
To your surprise:

Oh the power
That lies in reach
When we heed God's word
As we hear one preach.

To watch the Savior
Do His great work;
To save a soul

Through the new birth;
To wash away
The stain of sin;
To watch that soul
A new life begin:

Oh the power
That lies in reach
When we heed God's word
As we hear one preach.

The Real Gamble

Life is but a gamble,
And to live is to take a risk.
To win is never to give up,
And to lose is to completely give in.
If you never take a risk,
You'll never fight the battle;
And victory is only achieved
By those who fight.
Whenever you're knocked down
You should always get back up again.
Never let yourself stay down;
For to stay down is to lose.
Though we aren't supposed to
Gamble with our money
Which we daily earn;

Each time we enter into a relationship,
We gamble with our feelings
And take the risk
That we'll be hurt;
But if you dare to love,
You'll find someone to return it.

The Reason For The Light

When you're accustomed
To the darkness of the night
It is so easy to become blinded
With just a little light;
But once your eyes adjust
To the brilliance of its glow,
You'll actually become amazed
At what you'll come to know;
For light was sent
Into this world
To reveal what has been hidden,
So that man can see the beauty
Of the gifts that God has given.

The Reflection

When people dress so Holy,
As I see you do,
They manifest the purity
Of a heart that's true.
Their dress is then a light
That is both seen and heard;
For it is reflecting the voice
That's hidden behind the word;
And when the heart is pure,
And the ways are clean,
The walk of man is faithful,
Then the light is seen.
Heaven's glory is then revealed
To mere earthly men;
The God of Heaven glorified
In the very end.

The Revelation

While looking for the answer
To my deepest question;
Trying out almost
Every single suggestion;
Not one thing seemed to work.
It seemed like some kind of quirk.
When it seemed like all
Was just about lost,
And my last idea
I had just tossed,
A thought slipped through
My thickened skull,
At a time when my mind
Was getting real dull.
Popped out of no where,
Or so it seemed,
As if it was just
Some kind of dream.
It made everything
Begin to take on form,
And brought a calm
Into the midst of my storm.

Where did it come from?
What is the source?

This thought seemed to come
From some other source.
This thought had seemed
To set my mind at ease,
And definitely came
From outside of me.

The Revolution

Some revolt against system,
Some against regime,
Some against order,
Some against the mean;
But there is a revolution
That is going on,
That for the most part,
Goes on unseen;
For it is a battle
That is beyond this life.
It is fought in the Heavens,
Not with gun or knife.
This war that's going on
Is almost not even heard;
For it is being fought
Through the Spirit,
With the Word.
It's in man's imagination,
And it's in his heart
That this battle is fought,
Lost or won in part.
Although this battle may go on

In an unseen realm,
The victory is seen
Just as clear as on film;
And when defeat is felt
Just as real as rain,
It is then revealed
Through one's pain.
Though victory is the lot
Of the determined man;
Defeat is the end
Of the double minded stand.
This revolution
Goes on and on through life
In the unseen realm
Of mental and spiritual strife.

The Rich Lady

No one really knows the source
From which her wealth did come.
They could only speculate
As to how it all begun.
All they really knew for sure
Was that she was rich indeed.
They did not know that
It all started with a seed.
She'd sow a seed of love;
And then a seed of care.
She'd sow a seed of kindness
To someone unaware.
She'd sow a seed of mercy;
And then a seed of grace.
She'd sow a seed of blessing
To someone in disgrace.
You see, riches aren't found in money,
Nor in things we may obtain.
True riches we find through relationships
That sets our spirits aflame
With love and adoration
For a holy God above

Who wants to by His Spirit
Fill us with compassionate love.
So, as we sow some kindness,
Or perhaps some love and care,
He'll bless us with compassion
To give us strength to share
His desire to help the hurting
And those so full of pain
To heal them of their condition
And cleanse them of sin's stain.

The Road To Bitterness

The road to bitterness
Is paved with stones
That harden the heart
Through many wrongs.

One of these stones
That is so there
Is that of apathy
That just does not care
How anyone feels
About what they've done
For they're just glad
That they've won.

The road to bitterness
Is paved with stones
That harden the heart
Through many wrongs.

Another stone,
Wouldn't you guess,
Is that old stone
Of unforgiveness

That holds the grudge
And won't forget
"Til all is paid,
The price of regret.

The road to bitterness
Is paved with stones
That harden the heart
Through many wrongs.

A third stone
That's cemented in
Is that angry stone
That just won't give in
Until avenged
Is their right
To get even
Through a fight.

The road to bitterness
Is paved with stones
That harden the heart
Through many wrongs.
Those that walk
Upon these stones
Become a prisoner
Of each and every wrong,
For the pain
That each inflicts

Dictates to them
What kind of tricks
That they should do
In order to protect
Their selfish right
To their regret.

The Road To Hell

We cannot miss physical intimacy if we have never been physically intimate. Although we all have desires that spring up on the inside of us from time to time. These flames we can easily quench if we have never actually experienced their end. But once one begins to travel down the road of experience, these flames begin to burn hotter and hotter until one is utterly consumed with such desire that can no longer be controlled, but instead this desire begins to dictate to one's senses just what it wants. When this happens, one may just continually feed it with more and more of this type of experience. At this point one's carnal desires have become his lord and master. Many people begin to live their lives seeking out ways and methods to continually feed this uncontrollable, unquenchable flame of desire; until they find out that this is the very foundation that Hell is built upon. Sensuality is the road, which once one begins to travel down, it starts to slope gradually downward. This slope pitches itself ever so slowly steeper and steeper downward; until the soul traveling down its path actually starts to fall head on into Hell. By this time, there are no guaranteed exits. It starts ever so unnoticeably; just a glance and a smile, then some words and then a touch, next pitching ever so gradually downward until both parties are engulfed in the flames of desire. There are exit signs that occasionally appear, also warning signs are periodically posted along this road. Now, there is a certain pitch along a certain section of this road where the exhilaration level at which one is traveling actually becomes extremely exciting and a lot of fun, but this only lasts for a season though. Before too long, as the speed gradually increases, one begins to realize that he is trapped and cannot exit this road on his own. The downward momentum has become so great that one cannot turn around even if he wants to. Unless someone else reaches into his situation and intervenes, he just won't be able to pull himself out of this descent. Unfortunately, so many of us come to just such a place before we decide to call upon God. Although there were many exits along this road before; at this point in the road, there is only one exit left; and that is to call on the name of Jesus. And should one call, Jesus may briefly intervene to find out, should deliverance come, what one intends to do. Then if Jesus finds this answer to be worthy, He will deliver him; but if not, then one will be left to continue in his descent; for this soul will have just used up his last chance to avoid the fires of Hell.

The Scent Of Sin

Willingly, he went,
Being led by the scent
That enticed his soul to sin.

And as his pursuit was enacted
By this which he was attracted
He decided to give in;

But along this path
He incurred some wrath
And thought that it came from Him.

Unknown by this man
It was Satan's hand
That brought him to this end.

He was trapped unawares
Caught in the fowler's snare
Discovering the bondage of his sin.

As he pondered his act,
Desiring to get on the right track,
He sought for forgiveness again.

More willing to save and heal
Than to punish and deal,
God met him in prayer again.

As he recommitted his life
To forsake his sin and strife
God refreshed his soul within.

I guess the moral to this story
Is if want to live in glory
To sin's scent, do not give in.

The Sin Of Selfish Ambition

So many of us, in this hour that we live, are seeking for security within the context of human relationships; which, in turn, translates our responses to people and/or situations into merely the pursuit of acceptance by those men or women that we esteem. But this type of response is actually an immature attempt to become, in some cases, what God would possibly lead us into becoming anyway. There is a real danger to this type of behavior though, and that is in the impurity of our motivation. For if we try to produce righteous behavior for the mere purpose of pleasing men, it is merely translated into self righteousness, which the Bible refers to as "filthy rags" for it is stained with selfish ambition. Selfish ambition can become a poison to our spirit and eventually to the Church as a whole; so don't let it deceive you into thinking that by pleasing men of God or the Church as a whole that you are actually pleasing God; although when you do please God, the men of God and the Church will be pleased as well. We can become so caught up in this pursuit of getting as close as we can to our Elders or Pastors that we actually push God away. God wants to have a direct personal relationship with each and every one of us, not an indirect relationship that depends upon mere human acceptance. We must be careful not to deify our leaders;

because we are all frail human beings that make mistakes; for even the most spiritual among us has the potential to make a mistake. The deification of any man outside of the Man Christ Jesus becomes idolatry in the sight of God. And remember that God is a jealous God. He will not share His glory with any flesh, no matter how spiritual he is.

The Single Mom

The single Mom
Tries so hard
To meet the needs
Of her ward,
Those that look
To her for care
And expect her to
Her life share.

The single Mom
Finds life tough,
And fords ahead
Though times are rough;
For she must
Not only serve
Her family at home,
She must work.

The single Mom
Must face alone
Many hard trials,
For her man is gone.
She must continue
To forge ahead,
For her children now
Must be fed.

The Sound Of Life

The sound of laughter
When children play;
The sound of crying
An infant wanting his way;
These are the sounds
Of Life at its best.
Without these sounds
Is it worth all the rest?

The sound of bleeting
Of sheep in the wind;
The sound of belowing
Of calves now and then;
These are the sounds
Of life at its best.
Without these sounds
Is it worth all the rest?

The Temptation

Trying so hard to resist
What this my heart desires;
For this attractive young woman
Had really sparked a fire.
Oh the pain I feel inside
As this my desire burns.
Can I yet resist it
As my heart just yearns?
Oh so afraid am I
That I might just sin
Against my Lord and Savior,
Yet I have hope He'll win;
And keep this my soul
Rightfully in his place;
So I might yet win
In this life course race.
But then should I stumble;
Yes, then should I fall;
I know I have an advocate
Upon whose name I'd call.
I would cry out for His mercy.
I would plead for the Blood;

And call on the name of Jesus;
Asking for the crimson flood.
Oh the Blood of Jesus
That can cleanse each stain;
And lift up this fallen soul
To restore it once again.
And I know without a doubt,
He will answer my call;
For He loves the repentant heart;
And He loves the sinner's call.

The Time To Pray

Struggling hard
To find his way,
He would not take
The time to pray.
Stumbling here,
And stumbling there,
Loaded down
With so much care;
Though it was now
Late in the day,
He would not take
The time to pray.
Continuing down
This lonesome path;

Sometimes feeling
Satan's wrath;
Still burdened down
As he walked in the way,
He still would not take
The time to pray.

Please, take time to pray.

The Tomb Of The Unknown Soldier

A whole lot more
Lies buried here
Than just some
Old dry bones.
Memories of the past
Are here;
Shattered dreams of
Broken homes;
Some plans of what
Might have been
That were never
Realized;
Both the love
And vigor of life
That was once seen
In these men's eyes.

God alone
Would only know
How much
That we have lost;
For what is really
Buried here
Is how much
That war cost.

The Valley Of Vision

The burden of the Valley of Vision
For the soul of each man's decision
To decide to follow the Lord
Where ever the Spirit may forge;
Oh, the vision of man's limitation
Doesn't quite reveal his destination;
So, then faith is the only power
That can lift man's eyes to that mighty tower,
And view the ultimate end
Of those that walk in sin.

The yearning of a longing Savior
For the worship of those that waver
From the path that is narrow and straight
That will lead men to those pearly gates;
Yes, the vision of man's limitation
Doesn't quite reveal his destination;
So, then faith is the only power
That can lift man's eyes to that mighty tower,
And view the ultimate end
Of those that walk in sin.

The Warrior Servant

He serves through fighting;
And fights by serving;
For his fight is
All wrapped up
In his service.

★ ★ ★

The Watchman

Standing upon
This wall of prayer
Guarding the Church of God;
Praying in faith
Believing in
The promises of His Word;
Watching out
For enemy attacks
Against unknowing souls;
Trying to keep
Them on track
While pressing toward
Heavenly goals;
Having my loins
Girt about with truth;
Righteousness covers my breast;
Prepared with
The Good News of
The gracious Gospel of peace,
The prayer of faith
Being my test;
Wearing Salvation's

Obedient helmet;
Wielding the Spirit's great sword;
Standing firm
Upon His promises
That I've found
Within His Word;
Praying always
With all prayer;
Supplicating for all saints;
Praying for His Holy utterance
To speak with boldness
Not to faint;
Declaring the mystery
Of God's great Gospel
For which I watch tonight;
For I'm a watchman
On this wall of prayer
Standing ready now to fight.

★ ★ ★

The Way Of Christ

Christ showed us how to live
By showing us how to die.
Christ showed us how to give
By teaching us to ourselves deny.
Christ showed us how to love
By laying down His life.
Christ showed us the way;
And His Word became our light.
Christ showed us God's mercy
Through the sacrificial cross.
Christ became the ransom for our sin
Through His sacrificial loss.
Christ showed us how to win
By surrendering His will to die;
Then rose up from the dead
Showing us eternal life.

Christ showed us sensitivity
Through a life of reaching to bless
All that were around Him
Whose lives had become a mess.
Christ showed us how to rise
By showing us how to fall.
Christ declared that the humble
Are those that really do stand tall.

There Comes A Time

Once when you were young
And still in your prime,
God had begun
A work in you.
Now, there comes a day,
And there comes a time
When, at last,
The fruit is due;
But when that fruit
Does not appear,
There comes a time
To prune and tare;
And when that fruit
Is sick and poor,
There comes a time
To prune some more;
But if that fruit
Does not survive,
This tree cannot
Be left alive.
It's then cut down
For fruitless deeds;

Then replaced
By other seeds.
But should that fruit
Become fat and full;
There comes a time
To shake and pull;
Then once that fruit
Has been released;
There comes a time
Of rest and peace.

There Is A Time

If there would be a time,
And there would be a place
Where all of sin
Could be erased
All at once
With no doubt,
Never to return,
Or come about,
When would that be
That we could see
A time without sin
And man set free?

If there would be a place,
And there would be a time
When righteousness
Would truly shine
So all could see
The Heavenly road,
And then lay down
Their heavy load
To then climb on to
That Holy way;
For the path is seen
By those who'd pray.

There is a time,
And there is a place
Where all of sin
Will be erased
All at once,
No shadow of doubt,
Never to return,
Or come about.
'Twill be when time
Has ceased to be.
That's when man
Will then be free.

There is a place,
And there is a time
When righteousness
Will truly shine,
So all will see
That Heavenly road,
And have the chance
To lay down their load,
And climb up on
That Holy way;
For this path will be seen
By those who pray.

Therefore Come Boldly

"Let us therefore come boldly
unto the throne of grace,
that we may obtain mercy,
and find grace to help
in out time of need."
Hebrews 4:16

Many times you feel
You haven't the right
To come boldly
Before God's throne,
And you feel
That in your troubles
You are so all alone.

But you need
To understand that
His invite to come boldly
Is not prefaced
By how righteous we are
Or Holy;
But simply with
Our need of Him
To come and meet our needs.
With this in mind,
We should not be afraid
To come and bow our knees.

There's No One Quite Like Mom

She used to have such patience,
Much greater than that of Job.
She used to express a wisdom
That kept me on the go.
She seemed to understand
The greatest trials of life.
She also made for my Dad
Such a perfect wife.
When I look back
Over the years,
Now that I am grown,
I can't even remember
One little thing
That she ever did wrong.
I guess it's cause
When I look at Mom
And all the things she's done,
I see her through eyes
Of the purest love,
And remember only

The care and fun.
I guess if there's a reason
Why I've never settled down,
I've yet to find
Another woman
That can wear her crown.

These Are The Blessings

To hear the voice of God
And then respond in faith;
To see the light of His Word
Illuminating the way;
To feel the Spirit drawing them
Into that secret place;
To commune with the Father
While they seek His face;
These are the blessings
Of the children of God
Sent to give them strength
As through this world they trod.
To speak the word of faith
And then watch the Spirit move;
To repent of all sin
Then to see them all removed;

To abide in God's presence
As if connected to a vine;
To be filled with God's Spirit
As if drunk on a new wine;
These are the blessings
Of the children of God
Sent to give them strength
As through this world they trod.

Things That I Regret

There is a song that
While in Church
We do sometimes sing.
It simply states that
"I have no regrets"
Since Christ became my king.

But there are some things
I do regret
That concern my life in Him;
And through this poem
I'll tell you of them
So the light will not grow dim.

I do regret
Each time I missed
An opportunity to pray,
To seek to know
What Christ would do
In the context of each day.

I do regret
Each time I walked

By a soul I could have touched
And shown some light
Within his path
To show him God's great love.

I do regret
That word unspoken
When quickened by the Lord
Because I feared
What they would think
About this one
That simply just shared a word.

I do regret
Each selfish act
That sought for what was my own
Instead of pouring
Myself out
So that Christ could then be shown.

I do regret
That I have lived
So much of this life for me
Instead of seeking
Another's good
So that they could be set free.

I regret the times
When I was asked
To pray through some problem or quirk;

But failed to seek
A time to pray
Or ask God about this murk.

I regret decisions
I've never made
Due to the choice to procrastinate
Or put off conveniently
That decision unto a better date.

I regret these things
That I now see
God meant to do me good;
But because I felt
So unworthy
I merely misunderstood
That when God meant
To give to me
The opportunity to give,
He was merely
Trying to teach me
The proper way to live.

Thinking Back

Thinking Back
In memory of
Those that passed
On nine-one-one;
Considering what
Might have been
If that day
Had never come.
Could we have grown
Even more adverse
To the righteous path,
And eventually
Have incurred
A more devastating wrath?
What if,
On this day,
Only one year removed
The towers still stood
So tall and erect
As our attempt to prove
That we can live
Out our lives

Without the help of God?
Would we then grieve
His Holy heart
To invoke His chastening rod?
All that God
Would have to do
Is to simply wink His eye
To allow
Another nation to
Simply go a'rye,
And destroy
A major city,
Possibly two,
Then, my friend,
Consider then,
What on earth
Would we then do?

Thinking back
In memory of
That fateful day
Makes me grateful
That God inspired
Someone to just pray
That alerted
Angelic forces
To awaken Beamer, Todd,
Who would stand
Against his captors

To disrupt an enemy plot.

Thinking back
In memory of
All the heroic dead
That left their loved ones
To sacrifice their lives
To save another instead,
Not considering
Their own self
Worthy enough to save
Gave it all,
Both heart and soul
So valiantly and brave;
So let us think
Back upon these
With gratitude of heart
As we strive
To maintain the freedom
Others to impart
Godly attributes.

Thinking Of You

Thinking of you
I went to bed
And could not sleep a wink.
Thinking of you
I got up
To pray for your spiritual link.
Thinking of you
I got dressed
And went to the church prayer room.
Thinking of you
I prayed there
For your deliverance to come real soon.
Thinking of you
I spent an hour
Down on my knees in prayer.
Thinking of you
I felt God's presence
And how much for you He cares.

I have no doubt
That God heard
For His presence was so real;
And I know
That His answer
Will come real soon with zeal.

Holy character,
Righteousness, and truth;
To be sure
That these are
Implanted in our youth.

This Church Mouse

Behold how poor
Is this little church mouse,
Who roams all around
The little church house;
Eating one morsel
At a time;
Anywhere one
He can find;
Only to rush off
With a scare
When someone else
Shows up there.
Making his home
Inside a wall,
Where the ceilings are
Much too tall.

To run and play
At night he will;
For in the day
He must keep still;
Trying his presence
To keep unknown;
So as to protect
His little home;
For if someone
Finds out his place;
His little presence
They just may erase.

This Decision Fence

I wish I had a girlfriend,
Or maybe even a wife;
One that I could share with
The rest of my whole life;
And perhaps we could have a child,
Or possibly even Two
That we would raise together
The best that we could do.
Train those children to know
The wrong from the right,
And help them both to find
Their own destined flight.
Then maybe this life to me
could make some real sense,
And I could then get off
This decision fence.

This Game Where Shame Begins

Oh how can a man
Truly understand
The height and depth of sin
Unless he has been
A participant in
This game where shame begins?
Is it only the man
Who's delivered and stands
That can really understand the plight
Of a sinner who's trapped
And so overwhelmed that
He's almost totally lost his fight?
Or is it when a man
Has followed a plan
That has led him out
That he can feel,
Then pray with zeal
For the sinner that's losing his bout?

It's when you can place
Yourself in the face
Of the man that's trapped in sin

Is when you are ready
To be constant and steady
Enough in your fight to win,
And then plant the seed
To pray and intercede
For those lost and bound within;
For once in the disguise
Of God's heavenly eyes
Can you understand the nature of sin.

This Is The Struggle

This is the struggle,
The fight to overcome
All the inner voices
That want to be the one
To control the direction
That this life will take
And lead it down a path
That will be a mere mistake;
The struggle with desire
For an intimate companion
That will share this life,
And my love through romancing;
The struggle for a way
To make a future through a living,
So to live a life of ease
Capable of giving
To those who are much less
Fortunate that I,
The fact that I cannot
Makes me tend to want to cry;
The struggle with a need
To save what is yet left

Of material possessions
Not yet victimized by theft.

So, often there's the feeling
That life has not been fair
To rob you of opportunities
That could have helped you make it there.
To defeat all of these foes
That continually fight within
Takes a determination
To fight 'til the end.
You can't ever relax
At all in this inward fight.
That is, if you ever expect
For things to turn out right;
And even if your goals
Never do materialize,
The fact that you don't give in
Makes you the victor in your eyes.

This War That's Fought

Behold how true
The statement is
That God is love
And that love is.

Behold how false
Is the lie
Presented through
The satanic eye.

This war that's fought
Between these two
Involves the souls
Of me and you.

Each battle's fought,
Won, or lost
As we begin
To count the cost;

Then decide
To make our plans
To serve God
Or selfish ends.

If Satan can
Our hearts' deceive
We'll only seek
Ourselves to please;

But if truth prevails
Within our souls
We will please God
And He'll make us whole.

This Worry Disease

Tell me why you're anxious.
Is it because you're not sure
From where the next dollar's coming
Or what's in the future?
Or is it because
Your days are filled
With trouble and with pain;
And you feel like your soul
Is just one giant stain?

-Tell me, my friend-

Will anxiety show you
Just how to get free;
Or will it just magnify
This worry disease?

Anxiety's a master
That'll master your soul,
Rob you of peace
As it's taking control.
It'll tell you of things
That just aren't so;
So why are you anxious;
Or do you know?

Time And Eternity

Time is the place
In which we live
Where we must learn
How to give
Of ourselves
In loving sacrifice
So that others
Can live blessed lives.
The only blessing
That we must see
Is how we have
Set others free
To worship and praise
The King of kings
As well as to Him
All glory bring.

Eternity is the place
In which God dwells;
And we also know
That it is the
Ultimate destination
For each human soul.

★ ★ ★

Time Is Flying By

Time is flying by and so many are
Just continuing down this path that leads to Hell.
Just hear their cries as the time flies by;
Perhaps you just may feel to give out a loud yell,
Or maybe jump up and down,
Waving both hands,
Trying your best
To get them to understand
That the direction they
Are headed toward
Is much worse than
Any prison ward.
If we don't tell them
How will they know?

And if we don't tell them
We also may go;
For to whom much is given,
Much then is required.
No excuse is acceptable,
Not even that we're tired;
For time is flying by.

Time

Time,
That great deceiver,
Is trying to make me
Into a believer
That I've got time
To do this or that,
Play with the dog,
Or chase the cat;
But knowing what I
Must now achieve,
I cannot afford
To be deceived.

Yes time,
My friend,
Does not take sides.
It just keeps on flowing
Just like the tide.
So, don't think that time
Will be yet your friend;
For before too very long
We'll see time's end.

*Time's rushing along
To an appointed date
That not even one soul
Shall get to escape;
So, I cannot afford
To be deceived;
For I got too much
To yet achieve.*

Timely Attempts

Time,
And time,
And time again
I tried so hard
To be your friend;
But when my friendship
Had then been spurned,
I really felt like
I had been burned;
But though this burning
Has not yet ceased,
I still do not
Feel yet released;
So, I'll still try,
And try,
And try again
To see if you
Will become my friend.

★ ★ ★

Tis The Season

'Tis the season
To be Jolly;
But many are hurting
Because of the folly
Performed by men
Of degradation
That performed their acts
Of devastation
That not only enraged
This free nation
But alerted the whole world
Of their need of salvation,
To save them from
A tyrant's hand
That would rule this world
With selfish plans.

Yes, 'tis the season
To be jolly;
But many are hurting
Due to this folly;
So, while we rejoice

O'er God's precious gift
Let us remember
Those who are adrift
Due to the loss
Of family and friends
And pray for their comfort
To help them win
The victory o'er
Their grief and pain
And help them to
Start over again
In Jesus name.

To Aaron

Yes, you are very small
And do not yet see
All that God
Has given unto thee;
But in time,
As you then grow,
You'll come to see,
And yes, then to know
That God has given
Into your hands
Some special gifts
For which He plans
To use your life
For the common good
But until your time
You'll be misunderstood.
So you'll go through
Some hard times
Until you make
God's will thine.

Once you see
And know the truth
You'll seek the Lord
Throughout your youth.
By the time
That you are grown,
You'll know the path
That is your own.

To Angel

I know about the pain
You suffered as a child.
As your parents split apart,
Your emotions just ran wild.

I know about the anger
That rests within your soul;
And I long to set you free,
And make you fully whole.

I know about the questions;
Each time you wondered why
That life had to be so cruel
That it made you want to die.

My child, My child,
I know about the bitterness
That eats at you right now.
By now you must be curious
To know from me just how.

You see,
I was there when you were born;
And watched you as you grew.
I was there each time you cried,
Although you seldom knew.
I was there in your lonely times;
And the times that you were blue;
And as you read these few words,
I am still here for you.

I was there when you were hurt
By what others had done.
I was there when you believed
That life would never be fun.
I was there when things were hard;
And battles just couldn't be won;
And as you read these few words;
I still think you're number one.

I saw you as an infant.
I saw you toddle around.
I saw you as you started school.
I saw you pout and frown.
I saw you as your family cracked;
And your tears did hit the ground.
I saw you at your Grandma's house;
Your parents not around.
I saw you as you carried a child;
And when you wore that gown;

Took the vows of covenant
With witnesses all around.

You ask me how I saw all this;
Just where did I stand?
I saw it all from Calvary's Cross
Where I suffered as a man.

So, when your anger rises;
And bitterness tries to control;
And you want to be set free
From its evil hold;
Remember that I'm waiting;
Just to hear your call.
I'm standing ready to deliver you
Completely through it all.
Just cry out to me, My daughter.
You'll find I'm standing near
To give you peace and comfort;
And fill your heart with cheer.

All My Love,
JESUS CHRIST

To Be A Candlestick Maker

I've been a carpenter;
And I've been a baker;
But I refuse to become
A candlestick maker.
Perhaps let me be
The one to cause the spark
That would light the candle
To dispel the dark;
Or perhaps, I can hold
The candle as it burns,
And direct the path of those
That lost their way,
And desire to return
To the path that's narrow,
Or to the one that's straight
That will lead them to
Those Heavenly Pearly Gates;

But to be the One
To Make the candle stick,
I believe that place is reserved
For the Judge of the Dead
And of the Quick,
Which is who I serve.

To Be A Thief

To be a thief
In God's Holy book
You don't have to rob a bank
Like just any other crook.
You don't have to be an embezzler,
A burglar, or a con;
No, just hold back the tithe
And you have become one;
For you're not stealing
From a corporation,
A bank, or a man;
But you're taking money
From the pocket of a missionary
Struggling some soul to win,
Or possibly from a Pastor
Trying to help a widow
That spent hours in prayer
To help the Church grow;

Or maybe from an Evangelist
That might spark a revival fire
Possibly even in your own soul
If it wasn't for your desire
To save your own life
By trusting in the dollar
Instead of trusting Jesus
And of Him being a true follower.

To Be Alone

To be alone
As I move through life
I find within
A continual strife
For desire is there
For companionship
Enough that I
Think to quit,
Give up on life
And what it can yield;
But I'll hold up my faith
To be my shield.
Each year I fight
This battle in hope
That I might find
The strength to cope
With this life I must
Live all alone,
No companion that I
Can call my own.
I know that God
Is ever there;

And continually shows me
That He cares;
But my social needs
Are left unmet
By the lack of one
To call my pet.
No, not a dog,
A cat, or a bird;
No animal or rock;
Or even a shrub;
But a woman
That can my life complete
And fill this empty life with sweet.
God I can't
Continue to walk
From year to year
Your will to stalk
If in my life
I have this void;
No friend to love;
No wife to hold.
Your word says, Lord,
"It is not good
That man should be alone,"
And that's understood.

To Build A House

To build a house
Takes a whole lot
Of thought and plans,
Of land, a plot.
The foundation must be
Set in a firm place,
So that wind and storm
Won't it erase.
Exterior walls
Need to be thick,
Insulated right
Full and quick;
For when the cold
Or heat doth come,
The temp inside is
Kept nice for some.
The decor of this
House that you build
Need not attract
The royal guild;
But just be-speak
The feel of home;

So that the child
Longs not to roam.
So build your house;
And build it right.
Make all the joints
Construction tight;
So that the tests
Of time it pass;
And the length of your life
It might outlast.

To Inquire Of The Holy Spirit

When you feel your life is over,
And there's no time left to live,
You have nothing in your spirit,
No, nothing left to give,
And you have no direction
And not sure what path to take,
Then to inquire of the Holy Spirit
Is certainly not a mistake;
For the Spirit's guidance will be righteous.
No, He won't lead astray.
The heart that's broken and contrite
He'll always show the way;
For once the forgiver starts to move
On behalf of repentant hearts,
He buries every sin
Neath His blood to cleanse each heart.

Covering sin by forgiveness is what the Spirit desires
Along with filling every soul with a zealous fire
To burn away those things that distract the soul's attention
From the will of the Holy Spirit or even God's intention.

To My Beloved

You say all the right things. You never curse or swear. You don't go to bars, movie houses, or anywhere that would compromise your faith. When you go out from your home, you make sure you're modest in your apparel so you won't attract the attention of any unwanted suitors; but yet there is something missing. You don't ever miss a church service. You're there every time the doors are open. You wouldn't even think of missing Sunday School. You even bring a visitor now and then. But yet there is still something missing. You abide by all the standards of the local church. You even go beyond what is laid down by your Pastor. You keep your hair just right, your sleeves just right, everything in place. But yet still something is missing. Your standards are supposed to be a reflection of your inward character and the convictions that are produced by having a relationship with me; but you have turned them into walls and barricades to keep me out. They've become a place for you to hide. As long as you look right, talk right, and stay out of the wrong places you feel secure. You trust more in your standards than you do in your God. Your standards are given to you to protect our relationship, not to keep us apart. Why have you used them to lock me out? You use them as a defense against my wooing. You use them to cover your ears when I'm calling.

*You say, "I'm alright; I do all those things I'm supposed to."
But I say, you're not alright. I miss those times when you'd
spend hours with me in prayer. I miss those times when you'd
spend time searching my Word for something I'd show you.
You used to be so awed when I'd reveal my truth to you. But
now the busy-ness of your life has you caught up in its care as
if it has become your lover. You caress your busy-ness without
even giving me one thought. What happened to my Word that
said, "Acknowledge God in all thy ways; and He will direct
thy path." I want to direct your path and show you how to
handle those busy days. I would walk with you through them,
and direct each step; but you won't even enquire of me. I'm
sending you this warning. You're about to miss the mark of
my high calling; and when you realize you missed it; then you
will cry out to me. But you can come to me now. I'm waiting
and will guide you through. I'm waiting and will deliver you;
and we can have those times together, caressing each other in
prayer again.*

*All my love;
JESUS CHRIST.*

To Overcome

To overcome;
What does it mean?
Is it getting high enough
For you to be seen?
Or it just beginning to dream?
Are there steps To overcoming;
Or is that just
The way it seems?

To overcome means
To come over obstacles;
Small or large
Or even unseen;
Things like
Doubt or fear,
Depression or rejection;
Things like
Anxiety or confusion,
Unbelief or deception.

To overcome means
To have victory,
Not defeat;
Faith, not unbelief;
Truth, not deception;
And acceptance, not rejection.

To The Bishops

To my niece,
Miss Emily,
Who is so bright,
And full of glee:
God has been good,
So good to you.
You must stay with God.
To Him be true;
For the day will come;
And soon it will;
Temptation will come
For you to rebel;
But you must submit
To Papa's hand;
For in time
You'll understand.

To Erica,
My sister's first:
Your dreams just might
Like bubbles burst;
Unless you learn

Your life to plan;
Find God's will,
Not some man's.
Aim at the mark
Of God's high call.

Aim with your heart;
Then give your all;
For God has got
Great plans for you.
He's got a task
For you to do.
To my Sis,
With faith of gold:
Pray for your girls
To be firm and bold;
For in times ahead,
They'll face a lot.
They'll need your prayers
Against Satan's plot.
Teach them well
To live the Word;
And one day
They will be heard.

Now, to the Priest
Of Sister's home:
Keep on walking,
In faith be strong;

For God's light
Will shine on you;
If you'll just
To Him be true.
Beware of pride.

It will deceive;
And lead you to
Untruth believe;
So humble yourself
Before God now;
So you'll be ready
When He shows you how
To walk completely
In Holy light;
And to overcome
The Devil's fight.

To Unlock The Doors Of My Heart

To unlock
The doors of my heart
Would open me up
To the fiery dart;
But my burdens
Would then depart;
If I'd unlock
The doors of my heart.

If I'd unlock
The doors of my heart;
My old ways would
Have to depart.
Then I could find
That brand new start;
If I'd unlock
The doors of my heart.

If I'd unlock
The doors of my heart;
Then Red Seas
Would have to part.
I'd watch my enemies
Begin to depart;
If I'd unlock
The doors of my heart.

To Win Or Lose

To win or lose
Is all in a choice;
Whether to fret;
Whether to rejoice.
We can face each day
In hopeless despair;
Or choose to approach life
With a lot more care.
Taking on the care of others
Will really help you
Get beyond all the problems
That daily face you;
For when you are looking
To meet others needs,
You'll find that your soul,
The Lord, He will feed;
And you'll never have
A need greater than
God's Holy Providence,
God's Holy Plan.
The choice that determines
Whether you lose or win

Is a choice you must make
From deep within;
For self or others
Are you going to live;
The glory and praise
To God will you give.
To win or lose
Is all in this choice;
Whether to fret;
Whether to rejoice.

Tortoise Or Hare?

Are you going to be a tortoise;
Or are you going to be a hare?
Will you just go fast;
Or will you even get there;
Or will you stop and rest
Somewhere along the way;
Or will you stay vigilant
When you seek the Lord and pray?

✫ ✫ ✫

Transition

There was a time
So long ago
In the course of history
A nation was concieved
And then brought forth
Through the loins
Of one chosen family.
Abraham and Sarah,
Isaac and Rebekah,
And then came Jacob's clan
Over the course of four centuries
According to God's plan.
Though this Nation
Had been carried
In the womb
Of Egyptian sin,
Came the day
That this nation
Would be brought forth again
By miracles and signs
And many Divine wonders
That could only have come from God.

No magician
Nor soothsayer
Could match the
Mosaic rod,
That Living Word
Of the Almighty
Expressed through
Such a man,
As was called
And was chosen
By the Master's plan.
Moses held
The rod of God
In fear and humility,
Called of God
For Transition
To set God's people free.

Transition is a time
Or possibly a season
That deliverance is
For some unknown reason
Beyond the ability of man.
Yes, it is the time
When only God can.

Trees Of Righteousness

There once were some trees
In a great forest of green
That represented all
That was righteous and clean.
They all stood so tall.
They stood so erect,
And they all grew together
As if part of a sect.
They all stood together
In a place all their own
In one accord they were standing
Together so strong.
Now there came some men
To visit this forest of green
In search of some way
From their sin to come clean.
When they came across these trees
So righteous and green,
They searched through their branches
For something to glean.
In search of some fruit
In these branches above,

What they found was forgiveness,
Hope, and great love.
As they began
To partake of this fruit
They found that righteousness
Became their new suit.
The more that they wore
This apparel so clean
The more they acknowledged
Their branches were now green.

True Understanding

The Bible says many things;
And most of them are clear;
But there are some things
That aren't so plain
Unless the Spirit's near.
True understanding
Does not come
From reason or from rhyme;
But only comes
Through relationship
With the Lord through time;
For to view things
Through the flesh
Will just merely deceive;
But to view things
Through the Spirit
Will help you to believe.

Trust The Nails

To open the doors
Never before opened;
To try to find
New ways to soar
Above the average
And the mundane
To new heights
Of joy and pain;
For the higher you soar
Above all the rest
Can make the fall
An awesome test.
To climb the mountain
And cross the abyss;
To live in victory
With nothing amiss;
To believe for mercy
In the face of law;
To pass the test
Instead of fall.
The trials and tests
Of life will come.

You can count on this,
And believe this one;
But whether you pass,
Or whether you fail
Depends upon whether
You trust the nails.

Two Buds

Enclosed in a bubble
Of fear and rejection,
This bud would not open,
Not even one section;
For life had not dealt
The hand that he wanted.
In his mind he was tormented,
By rejection was haunted.
Withholding from the world
All his pomp and his splendor,
He kept to himself,
Not one service did he render.
What was the end
Of this bud that never flowered?
He was cut off and burned up
At the midnight hour.

Another bud on that
Same branch of the tree
Faced the same fears
And rejections as he;
Risked opening one section
At a time just to see;
Found the light of the sunshine,
Bright warmth and victory.
The more he opened up,
The more that he found
How beautiful life was
Once he was not bound.
As a flower looking back
To when he was budding,
Wondered why he had feared
To let one blade start to jutting.
Though fears and rejections
Of the past cloud your mind,
Open up to God
And His Church and you'll find
What you thought would just
Push you back in your shell
Are really the things He's sent
To help you get well;

For when you face fears
And rejection in life,
You gain faith and acceptance
In the sunlight.
So open up to God
And His Church this very hour,
And you'll find the beauty
Of being a flower.

Two Fires

Being a man
Of like passions,
I understand
Your desires;
How that you desire
Companionship sometimes
'Til it feels like a fire
Is burning on
The inside of you
Trying to take control;
But if you let it burn,
And then burn within your soul,
It just may consume you
From the inside out,
Until you're just out of control,
And losing this bout;
But you don't have to
Loose control of this desire;

But instead you can give
Yourself to another kind of fire,
Which is born out of seeking
After the most High God;
And will help you take control
While in this world you trod.

Two Prayers

The prayer of the heart
Is faintly heard,
Until expressed
With the word.
The prayer of the soul
Is crying out,
And will be heard
Without a doubt.
When will God answer?
What will God say?
Yes!
Amen!
Believe!
Today!

✫ ✫ ✫

Two Rings

One night,
A man had a dream.
In this dream
Someone had handed him two rings.
He was so taken by the sight of these rings
That he didn't really pay attention
To the one who had brought them to him.
One of these rings was an engagement ring,
And the other one was a wedding ring;
But there was something
Very different about these two rings.
They were not made of precious metals;
But they were actually made of a living vine.
This vine was gold in color
And had green leaves grouped in clusters.
Each cluster of leaves contained a diamond stone
That appeared as if they were some kind of fruit
That had been produced by this vine.
When he awoke, he began to be troubled by this dream;
At least until he received the understanding.

This is the interpretation.
Each ring represents a different level of relationship.
And the fact that these rings
Were made of a living vine
Let him know that these actually were
Levels of relationship with God;
For Jesus had once said,
"I am the True Vine."
One ring represents betrothal,
A level of commitment before covenant.
The other ring represents
Our marriage covenant with Jesus Christ.
The vine's gold color
Represents the faithfulness of God,
And the green leaves
Represent the fact
That Jesus Christ,
"The True Vine,"
Is the source of life
Within these two levels of relationship.
The diamonds, "or fruit,"
Represent the purity of God's grace and love
That flows from this vine.
The bearer of these rings
Is the Bride of Christ
Who Jesus is returning for
In the rapture of the Church.
The engagement ring represents

A repentant soul that
Has yet to take on the vows
Of covenant relationship.
The wedding ring represents
That soul after it has taken on the name
Of its Heavenly Husband,
"Jesus Christ,"

In the waters of Baptism.
The consummation of this relationship
Is the Baptism of the Holy Ghost.

U's

Ultimate Win

So, you've lost everything.
Your world has fallen in.
That, my friend,
Can be the ultimate win,
The time to start all over again.
Everything is finally gone;
Because everything has gone wrong.
All is lost, With one exception;
For you took one step
In the wrong direction.
Now, you and God
Is all that's left;
And your whole world
Has been victimized by theft.
Satan stole it all from you;
And you're left wondering
Just what to do.
The ultimate win,
My friend,
Is just you and God,
Once again.
So, stand up

To your feet;
And forget about
Your defeat.
Move forward.
Move on;
For God Almighty
Will make you strong.
You may think that you've lost;
But, my friend, you've gained
Another chance to succeed
By starting all over again.
You see,
Most people who win
Have lost time, after time,
And then after time again;
Before their faith,
Their perseverance
Pushed them over the hump again.
So you just may fail,
And fail, and fail again;
But success is inevitable
If you are determined to win.

Upper Room, If You Can

Upper room,
If you can speak,
Then tell us of
Those that weep
For loved one's lost
And dying souls,
And their desire
To make them whole.

Upper room,
If you can sing,
Then sing the songs
That warriors sing
When waging war
In heavenly realms
For new souls to win
And join in hyms.

Upper room,
If you can cry,
Cry out for those
That will soon die

Without the Lord
Making residence in-
Side their hearts,
New life to win.

Upper room,
If you can love,
Then love all who
Seek God above,
Whether for themselves
Or another's woes.
Just love all who
To you come and go.

Upper room,
Oh you can speak,
And sing, and cry,
And love the weak;
For you can speak
Through prayers prayed,
And sing through songs
By broken hearts made.

You can cry through those
That weep in prayer
For lost loved ones

And for others they care.
You can love through those
That love so much
Because they spent time
Seeking God to touch.

So, upper room,
Do speak, and sing, and cry aloud,
So that all who visit you
Can love the crowd,
The masses of people
That still do not know
The impact of love
By those that to you come and go.

★ ★ ★

Urgent Times

As time marches on,
And a new year begins,
The Church of the
Living God
Is faced once again
With this feeling of urgency
In respect to the times;
For She's one year closer
To Rapture Time.

As the days just pass,
Through a new beginning,
We find that we're closer
To this age's ending;
And we need to get ready
To see the clouds back rolling
As the revelation of Christ
In the air is unfolding.

Each day that the clouds
Cover the horizon,
I find myself just listening

To hear a trumpet blaring
Announcing the appearance
Of Christ descending
To catch the Church away
And begin time's ending.

V's

Valuable Lessons

Valuable lessons,
What we from them learn,
Pray Lord, let them in
Our memories burn,
And etch out a place upon our minds,
So when they're needed
We can easily find
The ones that relate
To our time and place,
And help us to run in this race.

Lord, let these lessons
That we must learn
Help us to
A better life earn;
And don't let us miss
Our opportunity
To find a way
To get completely free.

Valuable lessons,
What we from them learn

Pay greater dividends
Than what we could have earned;
For what is saved
On down the road
Will spare us from
A much heavier load.
If we'll learn these lessons
Right from the start,
It'll spare us pain
Down deep in our heart;
But if we fail to heed
The warnings they send,
We'll find ourselves hurting
All over again.

So, learn those lessons
That life sends to you.
Learn to be faithful.
Learn to be true.
Learn to appreciate
What life sends your way.
Learn to be thankful;
And then learn to pray.

Victory Road

Everyone deserves a chance at life,
Men to be a husband,
Women to be a wife.
They deserve a chance to live
In comfort and peace,
Not imprisoned by circumstances
With no sign of relief.
They deserve a chance to prosper
And to make life count,
Not to have the waters of life
Clog up at the fount.
They deserve a chance to be
What they truly desire to be,
And that is happy and content
And completely free;
But life can be so cruel
With all of its twists and turns.
It can leave someone wounded
With so many scars and burns.
It can literally throw you
For loop after loop,
Until you are standing dizzy,

Wondering what is the real scoop.
How do you deal with life
When it robs you of your chance?
Do you just keep on chasing it
Like someone to romance;
Or do you just give in to its wishes,
And succumb to its demands,
And let it trod you underfoot,
Like insufficient plans?
Do you throw yourself away
Like some garbage on the street;
Or do you get back up and fight
All the more determined to defeat,
And claim again another chance at life
To become what you are dreaming,
To fulfill your eternal purpose
That gives your life some meaning?

Get up,
Oh man,
Be strong,
Don't give in to life's demands.
Reach again for those dreams.
Set new goals and new plans.

Don't become a casualty
In this battle of life,
But stand in faith,
Believing that God
Will help you with your strife.
If you continue fighting,
Having your faith in God,
You will win eventually,
And the victory road you'll trod.

W's

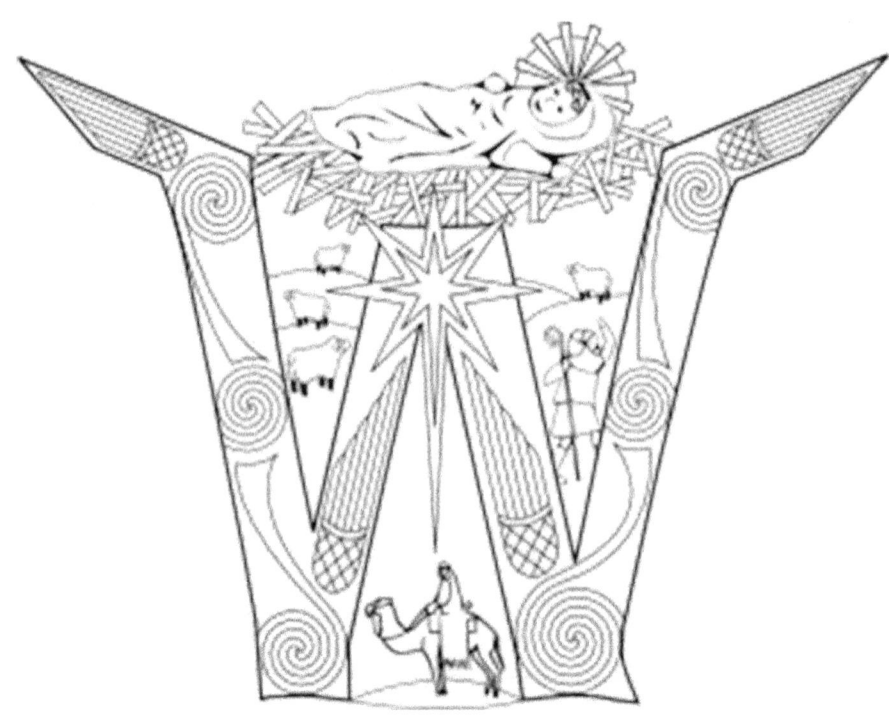

Waiting For You

Waiting for you
Has been so long,
That I thought I might
Have not been so strong
Enough to stay
Upon the road
Of the righteous
Til I'm old.

I'm glad to have
Finally found
That one true love
On this earthy ground
That I could spend
Out my days
With her giving
Our God the praise.

Now I'm waiting
For you my dear
So we can spend
Our days in cheer

*Living our lives
In full abundance
Doing God's will,
Not living redundant.*

*Though waiting for you
Is still so hard
I'll continue on,
Continue to trod
Down life's road
That's no longer odd
In faithful adherence
On Holy sod
To God's Word,
And the Spirit's prod.*

Walking In The Light

Walking in the light
Will expel the night,
And will expose the right,
Bringing victory to the fight.
Things will get real bright
And clear in our sight
When exposed to Jesus
Who is the true Light.

Walking in the dark
Will make vague the mark,
And may quench the spark,
Will cause dogs to bark
And confuse the lark,
And make it hard to park.

Making up our mind
Will help our way to find
Making it easier to bind
Ourselves to the right kind,
And will help the tension to unwind.

Walking With God

Walking with God
Can be a real test;
For sometimes you cannot
Walk along with the rest
Of your family or piers,
And sometimes this will last
For many, many years.

Walking with God
Can be a real trial;
For sometimes you won't be
Accepted for awhile
By the status-quo of
Those you hang around
'Til the fruit of your walk
Has been discovered or found.

Walking with God
Can be so fulfilling;
For when God uses you
In the process of instilling
Within someone's heart

An eternal hope,
You feel so grateful
That you're part of the rope

That has been extended down
To pull other souls out
Of the miry clay
Onto solid ground.

Warring Angels

Warring Angels standing ready
To do battle on our behalf.
They are awaiting one simple thing
Before they step into our fight.
They're listening for the desperate cry
Of hungry hearts and thirsty souls
Crying out to Jesus Christ
To be made completely whole.
They're watching for decisive steps
Toward the good and righteous path
Before they move into position
To express a Godly wrath
Upon the enemies of the souls
Of the many righteous saints
Expressing God's Holy Word
Authoritative to acquaint
Demonic forces with the power
Of the Holy One on high.
So, beware, Demonic forces,
The Kingdom of God is very nigh!
Angelic forces standing ready,
Swords all drawn, shields raised high;

Standing on the edge of battle
Listening for the battle cry.
Demonic kingdom, be thou warned,
And tell your leader,
"It won't be long.
Jesus Christ so soon is coming,
His banner waving, and waving strong.
He's coming for a bride that's waiting
Prepared and dressed for that day
That her bridegroom will come and get her,
Take her away though come what may.
He'll move the heavens, need it be,
To make this day view bright;
For He's coming soon in glory
Showing the way for He is light.
" Warring angels standing ready,
And ready now to fight
For the hungry and the desperate
To find their way into the light.

Watching From A Distance

Watching from a distance
This man from Galilee,
Seeing Him heal the sick,
Setting many people free;
Wondering if
There's enough
Power left for me.
Or should I even
At all attempt
To make it to His feet?

Oh, I'd better try
To reach Him now;
For there may never be
Another chance
To find out what
This man can do for me.

So, as I press on
Through the crowd,
An awareness grows in me,
How very bad

I need His touch
To secure my victory.

The more I press,
The more I feel
Determined to receive
This virtue and
This power from
This man from Galilee.

A few more steps
To reach Him now;
And most everyone can see
How determined
I have become
To reach my destiny.
One last reach
To touch Him now,
And just maybe I'll be free.
Just a little
Bit to stretch,
His hem is what I see.
I've touched Him and
I feel His power
Surging all through me;
Burning its way
Through my soul
Setting my soul at ease;
Purifying every fiber

Of my total being;
Cleansing my heart of all of my
Sin and iniquity;
Lifting that burden
That has been
Crashing down on me.
Now I know
That because of
This Man from Galilee
I can freely live
A brand new life
For Christ has set me free.

Watching Jesus

Watching Jesus life
As I turn each page;
Changing life after life;
Calming storms which rage.
"What kind of man is this?"
Is what Saint Peter said;
"Why He just spoke to the storm;
And now the storm is dead."
Never before had any man
Expressed such powerful words;
That even the common elements
Obey when they are heard.
Is it any wonder
That this man became
The central focus of history
With just the mention of His name.
Why, we even count our days
In reference to His time;
Yet His ways to men
Seem to be so hard to find.
Watching Jesus death
On the Cross of Calvary;

Watching such surrender;
Which is what really set us free;
Led as a sheep to slaughter;
Opening not His mouth;
Laying down His life for all;
East, West, North, and South;
At the end of life;
Forgiving all mankind;
Then giving up the Ghost;
So that we can find
A brand new start forever
Outside the bounds of time;
Across the Heavenly Jordan;
Eternal life to find.

Watching the resurrection;
Such power never known;
Just as if the husbandman
A corn of wheat had sown;
Pushing death aside;
As if it were a stone;
Coming forth
Up from the grave
So we won't fight alone.

What Can Rejection Do For You?

Rejection can give you a means where with you may identify with Christ, who, by the way, was "DESPISED AND REJECTED OF MEN." It can help you to develop a forgiving spirit, for if you never have anyone to forgive, you cannot learn the lessons of forgiveness. Once the lessons of forgiveness have been learned, rejection can then become a tool that you may use to enhance inward growth, thereby helping you to build emotional stamina that can only strengthen your character. The rejection of men can also help you to understand and appreciate the value of Divine acceptance, as well as the devastating nature of the adoption of the desire to please men as internal motivation to obey scripture, instead of allowing the concept of pleasing God to become that motivation. Rejection can also become a means of building your faith through the exercising of your faith in the overcoming of fears that are so often released into our lives through the rejection of men or women that we care about. As we overcome these fears we grow stronger in our faith toward God, for someone once defined fear as simply "THE ABSENCE OF FAITH."

What Do You Want From Me, Lord?

What do you want from me, Lord?
Do you want most of my time;
Or maybe, you want the knowledge
That you planted in my mind?
Is it possible you want my dreams;
Or perhaps, my life long plans?
Could it be you want my feet;
So you can help me make a stand?
Should I give to you my hands;
So you can work my messy life out;
Or maybe, you want my faith;
So you can chase from my life doubt?
Are you asking for my eyes;
So you can show to me the way;
Or should I give to you my knees;

So you can teach me how to pray?
Though Lord somehow I know
That you really want all these;
I kind-a-think my heart
Would make you the most pleased.

What Does It Mean To Trust The Lord?

What does it mean
To trust the Lord?
Does it mean that
You need to great rivers forge?
Or perhaps to
Give God His due?
Or maybe to sit weekly
On the same church pue?
Or could it be to climb
Up a mountain so high?
Or give to world missions
Til you're financially dry?
No, I believe
That to trust Him
Is just to believe what He says
And to take Him at His word
For all of your days.

What Fasting Does

Fasting does not move God;
But it does move us;
For God is already moving
And doing all the things
That we need.
But, for most of us,
We just are not
In the position
We need to be in
To receive from Him
What we need
Or to be used by Him
In the way we desire to be.
And fasting,
When it is done correctly,
Will move us
Into the position
We need to be in
In order to allow
God to accomplish
What we need or desire
Him to accomplish.

So if our need goes unmet,
It really is not God's fault;
But it goes unmet

Because we are not
In the right position
For His power to flow into
And through our lives.

What God Knows

What God knows,
He will reveal
To all those who seek
After Him with zeal.
When God reveals,
He will require
A response from a heart
That burns with desire
To be used by
His mighty hand
To reach out to help
Some fallen man.

So, if you want
To know God's truth;
Seek after Him with
The zeal of youth;
And He will reveal
The things you need
To help you reach the

One With the hands that bleed
For the sins of
Each and every man
To cleanse them from
The stain of sin.

What God Loves

God loves the tears
Of broken hearts
As they reach up to Him;
For then He knows
That He is welcome
To send down His Love to mend.

God loves the cry
Of broken lives
As they strive to bend;
For when they're bowed
Down to the ground,
Then His Grace can enter in.

God loves the struggle
Of broken men
As they receive His Word;
For He knows that
They can truly win
Once they've heeded what they've heard.

God loves the passion
Of broken spirits

Interceding for lost souls;
For He knows that
Once they pray through,
He can then make lost men whole.

What Is Truth?

"What is Truth?"
Someone asked.
"Is it the pulling
Off of a mask?"
"Truth," I said,
"It's not a what.
Truth, my friend,
Is a who.
For Truth is the one
That created me and you.
Oh and Truth is not an it,
As some would describe;
For Truth is Jesus Christ
Who's still looking for His bride."

What Now, God?

God,
Are You calling me to do
What You once told me not to?

Lord,
Are You reviving in me a promise
That I had once died to?

Jesus,
Are You moving me to a field
That You once pushed me away from?

As a young man I wanted to be a preacher of Your Gospel. I wanted to share Your Word with others. I do admit that at that time I had vested interests in my pursuit of this goal. I wanted to be accepted and needed by someone. I wanted and needed the security of friendship and/or fellowship. Now, it has been about 25 years since I preached a sermon, and frankly I have pretty much died to the hope of ever preaching again. I don't want to do it for the previous reasons. Those reasons are dead. I've tried so many things to prosper myself financially that I'm running out of options. Carpentry has failed to support me. Baking has failed to support me. Sales has failed to support me. Fast food has failed to support me, much less prosper me. So, I'm asking You, Lord Jesus, just show me, tell me, move me, direct me, anoint me, take Your hand and guide me in the direction that You want me to go. It doesn't matter to me what you do with me vocationally, whether it is warehouse work, computer work, frying donuts, or baking bread. It could be building homes, dog houses, or preaching the Gospel, singing, or teaching. Whatever you want me to do, Lord. I'll do it with all my heart as unto you. All I ask, Lord Jesus, is that You lead the way; You walk with me through it, and confirm Your Word with the appropriate signature of Your glory. All I need, Lord, is You guiding me, You empowering me, and You accenting my work for You with Your presence. If You are calling me to preach now; please make it absolutely clear to me and to my Pastor. Perhaps all You wanted to do is show me the difference between the desire to preach and the call to preach. Or perhaps You do have another ministry, more in the line of music and/or teaching.

What Really Matters

When the end is near;
And you are sure
That your life is ready;
And your heart is pure;
Then what really matters
Is not all your things
And the pleasure that
They might bring;
But that you
Really know the Lord
And are prepared
For your eternal reward;
How many lives
That you touched down here
While traveling this world
As a mere stranger.

★ ★ ☆

What's In A Name?

"What's in a name?"
He asked.
I said,
"Depends upon the name.
Jacob was a deceiver.
Israel was a prince.
Saul was a murderer.
Paul was an Apostle.
So, what's in a name,
But strength of character,
The definition of a life.
Take the name of Jesus.
In that name there is
Salvation, deliverance, healing, peace,
Faith, truth, mercy, love,
And anything you need
Jesus to be to you."

What Shall I Give Jesus For His Birthday?

When I consider the question
Just posed before me,
"What should I give Jesus
For His birthday?",
I must look
In His Holy book
In order to discover
What He has already
Received from others.

On the night
Of His Holy birth
Though it wasn't even
Near what He was worth,
Some shepherds came by night
To bow in His Heavenly sight.
Though these men weren't rich
In material possession,
They offered up their hearts
Filled with adoration.

Then when He was two
Wise men came from afar.
It took them some time
To follow that blessed star.
They acknowledged Him as king
And offered him their gifts,
Myrrh, gold, and frankincense
Were among their lists.
Again here the value
Did not even approach
How much He would offer
A world full of reproach.
Now, I truly understand
That nothing I could give
Would not ever compare
To God's heavenly gift.
The only thing I can give
That to me even makes sense,
To make myself available
To be filled with His presence,
An offering not of money,
Not of material wealth,
Nor a life with status,
In perfect physical health;

Nor an offering of
Great material possessions,
Or of a life of influence
With rulers in succession.
All that He requires
Of any of His children,
Is to yield to Him our lives
In order to build His Kingdom.

What Time Is It?

What time is it
When time has run out?
Would it then be time
To get rid of doubt;
Or time to see
Your life and just pout
About the fact that
Time has just run out?

★ ★ ★

What To Do With Blessing

What to do with blessing
Can be hard to comprehend
When it seems like it's intended
To fill a void within;
But consider how God blesses
In abundance and much more
Until we're overflowing
With an abundant store.
God never intends for blessing
To feed our inner lusts;
For it's really God's intention
That we put others first.

So, don't ever hoard your blessing,
And use it for selfish gain;
For by just storing up your blessing
You may incur a stain
That'll keep future blessings
From ever coming your way.
Yes, selfishness can cause
The blessing to stay away.

What We Should Desire

To be used
By Almighty God
To save this world
From the chastening rod;
This is what we should desire;
To be set aflame
With Heavenly fire;
To burn as a candle
In the dark of night;
Sharing with others
This Heavenly light;
To walk in paths
That are narrow and straight
That will lead us right to
Those Pearly Gates.

What You Need To Know

I'd like to take you out sometime
To get better acquainted would be fine;
But there is something about me
That you should know;
And that's that I
Don't belong to myself although.
There are limits to my life, you see.
I'm bound by chains of liberty.
Years ago, I made this choice,
To serve the Lord with one voice.
Total allegiance to the King of kings,
To live for Him and His praises sing.
Don't think me weird if I refrain
From carnal pursuits and sinful stains.
I'm just trying to live for God,
And worship Him while through this world I trod.

Yes, I'd like to take you out
So we can get better acquainted;
Of this there is no doubt;
But please do understand,
This is the life that I choose.
It was and is my choice
Not to be loose.

What Your Presence Means To Me

What does Your Presence,
Oh Lord,
Mean to me?
It means life,
And liberty.
It means hope,
And to be free.
It means love,
Joy, and peace.
It means there shall be
Many new releases.
It means righteousness,
And law.
It means that my life
Will be worth living
After All.
It means provision,
And satisfaction.
It means that my life
Won't just be a reaction.
It means purpose,
And fulfillment

It means my life will have
A Divine in filling.
It means power,
And authority
Over things or spirits
That desire to have control of me.
It means that my eternal destination
Will be to spend Eternity with
The Lord of all creation.

What's Hidden In The Shadows?

Lurking in the shadows
Of many past experiences of our lives
Are the hidden voices
Of fear, doubt, and unbelief,
With which we all strive.
While God's word declares
That "The Truth shall set you free",
These little voices hide
Behind past hurts, disappointments,
And the traumatic experiences
That each of us have endured.
So we not only need
God's light of Truth
To shine on those experiences;
But we really need it
To permeate the darkness
Contained within these shadows
If we ever expect to be totally free.
It is just intolerable for us
To allow these shadows
To continue to exist during this End-Time Age.
We just can't continue

To allow hiding places
To remain within us
As pockets to which
These voices can escape.
In order for us to do battle
With these voices
We must open ourselves up
To the scrutiny of the Holy Ghost
In prayer and fasting
By allowing the Spirit of God
To thoroughly purge our hearts
Through an internal investigation
Of our personal motives.
The work of the Kingdom of God
Is far too important
To allow our petty vested interest
To become the catalyst
That aborts God's plan
For our individual lives.
There is just too much at stake.
God's will and plan
Must be the ultimate goal
Of each and every one of us,
No matter what
You or I want or have to do.
The cost of doing God's will
Is virtually everything
We are or ever hope to be.

This is the Cross
That we must bear:
"The presentation of our bodies
As a living sacrifice;
The total destruction of our own concept
Of our future in this world;
And complete submission
To God's will and purpose for our lives."

What's The Use

"What's the use?"
Is what the voice said,
The words of an attitude
That would keep me down instead
Of allowing me to try,
And then try again
Til I cross over
Into Victory Land.

"What's the use?", I said
In response to this.
"Why there are souls to reach,
Encourage, and to even bless.

There's also a reward
That's awaiting those
That faithfully stand,
Even on their toes,
Ready to fight
The good fight of faith
By reading the Word,
Then meditate and pray
Seeking the Lord
With a fervent spirit,
Determined to find
His voice and hear it,
To follow the leading
Of the Spirit's call,
To lay down their lives
And surrender all.
The promise is this,
From the Holy Word:
It will be worth
Enduring the sword,
The trials of life,
Misery's plight.
It shall be worth
The daily fight.
Though victory seems
A distant land,
By God's grace
This gulf I'll span.

Though I may fail,
And fail again,
I'll keep on fighting
Til I can stand
Firmly upon
The Word of faith,
View God's moving hand,
Receive God's grace.

When A Man Is Tempted

When a man is tempted,
Is it from within,
Or from outside of him
Does this temptation begin?

Does it begin with a smile,
Or maybe with a flirt;
Or does it begin with a lady's
Short, short mini skirt?

The heart of man is wicked
In what it can imagine;
And when it comes to sin,
It is ready to take action;

But in order to follow through,
This man,
He really must choose
Whether to be a conqueror of sin,
Or to sin lose.

Though the heart of man is wicked
And his thoughts be impure;
Unless he is enticed,
This man, He can endure.

When God Speaks

When God speaks
With an audible voice
To bring to one's attention
A much better choice,
One tends to listen
To His every word;
For His audible voice
Is rarely ever heard;
For that God usually seeks for
A demonstration of faith
By all those who feel after
The right life course or race.

But there are times when
A particular life will affect
So many other lives
That God chooses to speak direct,
As with Moses, Samuel,
And the Apostle Paul;
For these men have been used
To direct us all.

When I Looked Behind

When I looked behind me,
Just what did I see?
Lots of lonely times,
Pain, and agony;
Rejection of piers,
And of those
That I thought did matter;
Just then to find that
In front of me was
An Eternal Latter.
So, I climbed up a rung
And found me some peace;
Up just two more
And found a brand new release.

The further up I'd climb,
The more I did discover
Of a power great enough
Any sin to cover;
Eventually to start looking
Up ahead and not behind;
For God's Divine acceptance
Is what I then desired to find.

When Life Begins

When a seed
That is planted
In the ground
Begins to sprout;
It is because
The hard outer shell
Broke wide open
Allowing new life
To then spring out.
Next that sprout
Presses on
Toward the surface
To find the light of day.
It pushes aside
Great big clods
Of both soil and clay.
So, by breaking the ground,
It makes this statement,
"I am here to stay."
You see,
Life begins for the seed
When the shell becomes brittle and broken,

Giving way to the force of life
As God's Word had once spoken.

Life breaks the mold
Of the form of death
Allowing a new course to be set;
So that life
Can start anew,
And needs can then be met.

When Sleep Escapes

When sleep escapes you
What should you do?
Just lay there and think;
Or get angry and stew;
Or should you attempt
To make this time productive,
Before your heart
Can become seductive?
Get up and read.
Get up and pray.
Get up and do
What you put off that day;
For once those things
Finally get done,
Sleep can then come to you.

Now, won't that be fun?
The fact that you
Cannot yet rest
Just might mean
You haven't done your best
To accomplish what
That day you needed to do;
So that sleep then
Can come to you.

When Weakness Becomes Strength

There was a common man
That was plagued with sin
That could not in his own strength
Fight the battle to win.
When he would give it his all
It never seemed quite enough.
To overcome this wall
To him was much too tough;
Until he met the Savior,
Jesus the Nazarene,
The one who went to Calvary,
And died for you and me.
Once this meeting was over
He found such strength through Him,
His life was changed completely
Including his struggle with sin.

As he learned to pray in the Spirit,
And read God's precious Word,
He did increase in wisdom,
And learned to wield the Sword,
That Word of Truth that's mighty
To the discerning of spirit and soul.
It really wasn't very long
'Til he was completely whole.

Where Does Back Sliding Begin?

Where does back sliding begin?
Does it start with a word,
A deed, or a sin?
Or does it start with a decision
Made down deep within?
As I look o'er
Many seasons of my past,
Those seasons when faith
Slipped from within my grasp,
I see a common thread
Woven within the core
Of each of these seasons
When faith from me was torn.
It's the thread of self interest,
The preservation of me
That seems to be present
During each one of these.
It's when I became concerned
About saving myself
Is when I began to loose
My spiritual health.
But once I'd abandon

My own preservation
Is when I'd experience
Spiritual restoration.

So, at the root of each
Back sliding of my life
Was a selfish motive
That caused me much strife.

Which Way Is Right?

Which way is right
When all the roads
Lead you astray?
Well isn't this
One of those times
Where the Lord actually
Makes for you a new way?
For He does make
For us a way
When there is no way;
Just like when Israel
Was standing by the sea;
God parted the waters
To set them free.

Which Way To Heaven?

"Which way should I go
To get to Heaven?" He asked.
"Do I turn right,
Or left;
Do I go slow,
Or fast?
When Do I know
That I'm on the right road;
When the road is rough,
Or smooth;
When light or heavy is my load?
I'm searching and hungry
For the true way,
And willing to go
What ever men say.
Should I stand,
Or sit,
Or should I kneel to pray?
Please, tell me;
Oh, tell me;
Yes, tell me today!
I told him that there

Is only one way he should go.
That's say, "Yes" to Jesus Christ;
To Him don't say, "No".
Follow Him to the Cross
Of Calvary, my friend.
Then follow on,
And on,
And on to the end.
He'll lead you and guide you
Each step of the way,
As you humbly talk to Him
In your prayer each day.
Walk with Him through the water,
And then through the fire;
And Jesus will clothe you
With Heavenly attire.
If Heaven is where
You're looking to go,
Then my friend,
Follow Jesus;
For the way
He will show.

You see,
He's the light
That's lighting the way;
And the way that you go
Is to reach out to Him and pray.

While Looking For Jesus

While looking for Jesus,
I searched and I found
Traditions of men
In this world all around.

When them I would try
I would then find
They could not fill
This void inside.

While looking for Jesus
I searched and I found
Religious men
In this world all around.

When them I would try
I would then find
They could not fill
This void inside.

While looking for Jesus
I searched and I found
The pathways of sin

In this world all around.

When I would try
I would then find
They could not fill
This void inside.

While looking for Jesus
I searched and I found
A highway of holiness
On higher ground.

When it I did try
I then found
I was filled with His presence
And true peace of mind.

While looking for Jesus
I searched and I found
A river of living water
Springing up deep within.

When it I did try
I then found
A spiritual refreshing
And a renewed mind.

White Castle

Living in a world of little white lies,
Is living within a delicate disguise.
One slip of the tongue
Can be so revealing
As to shed enough light
To stop the congealing.
Where does truth start?
Where does truth end?
How big is the lie
With which you defend?
Woe to the man
In this little white castle;

For when truth is revealed,
Oh, how will he wrestle
To try to convey
The validity of the lie;
But his world is just standing
On shifting sands in disguise.
So my friend if your world
On truth is not found;
Don't be surprised if eventually
It comes crashing right down.

Who Can?

Who can withstand
When God's mighty hand
Moves?

Who can sin hide
When His all seeing eye
Proves?

Who cannot feel
Whenever God deals
True?

Who will not pay
When God says, "Today,
It's due"?

He is omnipotent.
Almighty God is He.
He is omniscient.
There's nothing He cannot see.

He's omnipresent.
Everywhere He will be.
He is the one true God;
And He'll work sovereignly.

Who Would Of Thought?

Who would of thought
That preacher man (Noah)
Who built an Ark of wood
Would spare eight souls
From the destruction of
An angry worldwide flood?
Who would of thought
When Abram walked
Following that still small call
That his seed would become
The focal point
When God decides to end it all?

Who would of thought
That shepherd boy (David)
Would be anointed King
Of the Holy Nation of God
And appoint singers to sing?

Who would of thought
That Daniel would
Emerge from the lion's den
Or Shaddrach, Messhach, and Abednigo
Would emerge from
Their fiery pen?

Who would of thought
A child that was born
In a stable one Holy night
Would affect every man on Earth
Whether they lived
Wrong or right?

Who would of thought
A dozen men
Would turn their world up-side-down
By praying in an upper room
Until Spiritual rain came down?

Who would of thought
One little man (Paul)
Would reach his known world
Before his head
Would be chopped off
For what he had unfurled?

Who would of thought
A couple that moved (the Manguns)
To Louisiana's central part
Would build a Church
That would reach around the globe
With prayer, gifts, and heart?

Who's Really In Control?

Being in control
Of how your life will be
Is merely an illusion,
And a lie, you see;
For life is actually controlled
By laws and principles
Set in motion by Almighty God
Generations ago.

According to the Biblical design
There's only two destinations;
Heaven and Hell;
The choice is our decision;
And if you think
It doesn't matter
The lifestyle that you live;
Then you'll be surprised
At the end of your life
When to death you yield.

Who's Birthday Is It Anyway?

"Away in a manger
No crib for a bed,"
Does that mean that Jesus
Arrived on a sled?
"Leading captivity captive,
Giving gifts unto men,"
Does that mean
He climbed down chimneys
With all sorts of toys and things?
On that first Christmas morning,
When those shepherds came,
Did they give each other gifts,
Or just worship His name?

And when those wise men arrived
From a journey so long,
Did they draw names,
Or sing each other a song?
Just tell me, my friend;
While you're listening in;
Just whose birthday is it;
Please tell me, my friend.

Why Complain?

I had wherewith to complain
And felt I might buckle under the strain;
But when I spoke my complaint out,
The pressures increased,
And I did pout;
And when my pouting was then all through,
Not one thing had changed,
But I was left blue.

Complaining never helps a thing.
It just magnifies the problems it sings,
Until overwhelming situations become,
And the defeat is felt much greater then some.

Now when I have wherewith to complain,
I don't consider the weight or the strain;
But try to see what I might glean
From the experience of this situation or thing;
For if I can learn,
And then can grow
In my knowledge of life,
So then come to know
How to cope with things
To enable me to be
A helping hand
For others like me.

Why Have I Waited?

Why have I waited
Oh so very long
To pursue a relationship
With some woman?
Is this because
Of inner fears
That kept me from this
All of these years;
Or is it because
Of God's purpose or plan
That I am still
A single man?
If I'm afraid
Of what life would bring,
Please, show me, Lord,

So that I can wing
My way to freedom
Through steps of faith
to help me find
My destiny or fate,
That one designed
By you for me.
Oh please, my Lord,
Set my soul free.

Why Worry?

Why worry about tomorrow,
When today is trouble enough?
Why worry about tomorrow,
When today is sort-of-rough?
You see, the things
You might then do
May not even
At all come true;
But the things that
You do today
May drive tomorrow's
Troubles away.
So, why worry about tomorrow,
When today you've got time to pray?

Why?

That's the question
That everyone asks
And no one understands.
In times of tragedy or loneliness
We just can't seem to cope;
Because we just don't have that one answer.
But let's consider one thing:
God, in His infinite wisdom,
Knows the way that we take,
And sees every unanswered
Question in our hearts.
Sometimes He chooses to give us the answer,
And sometimes He chooses
To let us go through a situation
Without a direct answer.
It is in those times
That we learn to lean
On His Everlasting Arms,
And trust Him to carry us through it.

We may desire an immediate,
Undeniable answer from God Almighty;
But God knows what we need,
Even if it isn't what we ask for.
And so, in those times,
Trust Him, who sees all,
For He knows what is best
For us all.

Windows

When they're open
They let in the breeze
That blows so gently
Through the trees.
When they're closed
They keep out the rain
Of those storms
That can cause much pain.

★ ★ ★

Wisdom Is Available

Wisdom is available
Unto the prudent man
That diligently seeks for
Understanding in everything.
But wisdom fleets away
From the slothful soul,
That just waits around
Never attempting any goal.
Whenever a man is diligent
In seeking after knowledge;
He digs deep to find it,
Then applies it like a wedge.
The slothful man is not interested
In ever coming to know
Anything that might mean
That he would have to grow.

For growth in the knowledge
And wisdom of life
Would place demands upon him
To stretch and to strive.
But there is one thing that this
Slothful man won't find;
Is that diligence would insure
A fruitful and productive life.

Wisdom?

Unlike some would believe,
Through academic study alone,
Wisdom is not received.
If you would desire to be wise,
Just look to Jesus Christ,
See life through His eyes.
Look at the suffering and the pain
That He had to endure;
Then look at the Holy Ghost rain,
And the joy set before.
Understand;
He did not have to
Give His life for us;
But He really wanted to;
For that He really loved us.

Wisdom counts the costs
Before making the decision.
Then knowing what is lost
Is only an incision;
Understanding the reward
Is much greater than the cost;
And the joy set before
Is much greater
Than what is lost.

With His Help

God is not as interested
in what you are;
As in what you can be
With His help.
God is not as interested
In what you are doing;
As in what you can do
With His help.

For with His help
You can be
A life changer;

And with His help
You can do Greater things;
And with His help
You can save
A soul from danger;
And with His help
New life to
Someone bring.

Woman Of God

The radiance of her countenance
Was far beyond compare,
Because that in her heart
The love of God was there;
For as she came to know
That God had first loved her,
She grew to appreciate
What had been extended to her.
The more she realized
The depth of this great love,
The more her heart did turn
Towards Almighty God up above.
The peace and confidence of knowing
How much God loved her
Shown as a bright and shining light
Toward those all around her;
And when people would then ask
The reason for this glare;
She would respond with,
"Its Jesus You're seeing inside here."

Wondering

When I sit
All perfectly still,
Wondering if
I'm in God's will,
I think about all the times
When His will I did not find.
Then I think of all the ways
That my failures can be praised;
And before too long,
In despair,
I find myself
Wholly there.

But when I'm busy;
And a'doing
All the things
That I'm knowing,
His light's a'shining,
His Word's a'showing
The very way
I should be going.

Word Lamp

Word Lamp,
Provide the light
For the path of my feet
So that this soul
Can see the way
To avoid the snares so steep,
And find solid footing
On higher ground
That leads to Heaven
So sweet.
So, Word Lamp,
Provide the light
For the path of my feet.

★ ★ ★

Words Of A Frustrated Prophet

Over whelmed
With frustration
About what to do
With a nation
Who forsakes God
For sensation,
The old prophet said,
"Understanding
The cost is great;
But for us,
Is it too late?
Did this country
Make a BIG MISTAKE?"

Rambling on in his bed,
"Are we doomed
For destruction
For our latest infraction;
Or can we still
Receive instruction,
And possibly
Take some action?"

Words

Words can be so right.
Words can be so wrong.
Words can be so weak.
Words can be so strong.
Words can be so false.
Words can be so true.
Words can make things old.
Words can make things new.
What is it that determines
How our words will be?
But how that they are used
By you and by me.

Words can be so blunt.
Words can be so kind.
Words can make you see.
Words can make you blind.
Words can be deceptive.
Words can be straight too.
Words can be real helpful.
Words can hinder you.
What is it that determines
How I words will be?
But how that they are used
By you and by me.

Words can be real smart.
Words can be real dumb.
Words can be real serious.
Words can be real fun.
Words can be real nice.
Words can be real mean.
Words can be real dirty.
Words can be real clean.
What is it that determines
How our words will be?
But how that they are used
By you and by me.

Words can be caring.
Words can also hurt.
Words can be sharing.
Words also can be curt.
Words can be real dull.
Words can be real sharp.
But one thing is for certain,
Words come from our heart.
What is it the determines
How our words will be?
But how that they are used
By you and by me.

Worry

Worry
Occupies space in the mind
Meant for something else,
Denies one the ability
For total concentration,
Is listed by doctors
As one of the primary causes of ulcers;
And we are commanded
By the Scriptures
Not to do it;
But worry has become
A common, undeniable failing of mankind.
Thousands have ulcers
From constant worry.
Mental institutions are filled to capacity
Because of worry.
Marriages have broken up
Because of worry.

Worry, My friend,
Is misplaced concerns;
For when you are concerned

About the things you shouldn't be;
You cannot be concerned
About those things that you should be.
Echos of worry
Drown out the voices
Of the concern
For the needs of others.
Worry, itself, is a thief;
For it robs you of:
Your intellect,
Your sanity,
Your health,
And your social life.
You see, you use energy to worry
That could be used more effectively
For more positive endeavors.

Writing Songs

Writing songs,
And a little prose
Helps me feel
Like God's real close;
For to feel
This inspiration
As it flows
Through my mind;
Then to write
This inspiration down,
So to preserve
It in time;
So that others may feel
That His Spirit is real.

Yes, I know that
All inspiration
May not be divine,
So, that's why I focus
On the Biblical kind.

X's

X-tra, X-tra

Extra, extra,
Read all about it.
Sins are forgiven
By the blood of Lamb.
Extra, extra,
Read all about it.
Man's debt is paid
By the Great "I AM".
No, not in the paper
That comes to your door;
But in that Holy Book
You neglect all the more.
The media won't report this
Good News of God's grace;
For their main focus
Is on man's disgrace.
So, turn in your Bible
To get the Good News;
And read it until
God changes your views.

Extra, yes extra,
Read all about it.
Sins are forgiven
By the blood of the Lamb.
Extra, yes extra,
Read all about it.
Man's debt is paid
By the Great "I AM".

Y's

Yesterday's Dreams

There's not a thought
Like yesterday's thoughts
That's full of the plans
Built upon hopes
And built upon dreams
Of what each new day
Could actually bring.
It was when we dwelt
On Yesterday's dreams
Is when we had hopes
Of what the future might bring.
Now that yesterday
Has since passed away,
What has become
Of yesterday's dreams?
Have they come to pass
Or just vanished away;
Or have they remained
A dream 'til today?
Are we pressing on
Through the passing of time,
Still pressing with the Hope

That our dream might still shine;
Or are we discouraged
And sitting at ease
Allowing anxiety
Our minds to just tease?

You Are My Reason

Lord, You are
My reason
For living.
Yes, You are
My reason
To be.
Oh, You are
My hope of
Salvation;
For through You
I have been
Set free.

You Can Become

You can become
A life changing experience
For the next soul
That you meet.

Oh, you can become
A kind of deliverance
That'll shine the light
For someone's feet.

Oh, you can become
A source of great comfort
For someone
That's filled with grief.

Oh, you can become
A life changing experience
For the next soul
That you meet

You Think Yourself Lonely?

So, you think yourself lonely and you feel so alone. You think no one cares; and you're out of the zone. Well, consider living forever past without even a single soul That you can confide in while you're resting or on the go. Consider looking across the great expanse of space Without the sight of one planet, or even one single face. Before God made this world, much less the first man, Consider God was lonely until He conceived His plan. First, He made Angels to appease this great need; Then made this world before forming you and me. So, when you are feeling lonely, consider yourself blessed To be allowed to identify with the Almighty at His best.

3's

Zeal

"Z" is for ZEALOUSNESS
For the worthy cause of Christ.

"E" is for ETERNITY,
A good reason to live just and right.

"A" is for the AUTHORITY
Of the Holy God of Heaven.

"L" is for the LOVE OF GOD
That will drive out all the leaven.

Acknowledgements

Firstly, I must give glory and honor to Jesus Christ, without which this book would not have been written. You see, He is my primary focus and inspiration. Secondly, I want to say thank you to some special friends, whose words of encouragement were not only timely but necessary for me bringing this project to completion. A special note of thanks to Sister Vesta Mangun and all my friends at the Pentecostals of Alexandria for helping me to realize the value of my gift from God.

My Testimony

All through school I sought one thing, to be accepted by the status-quo; but did not find that blessed thing; but tried really hard although. I got into fights, not once or twice, but nearly every day. T'was no fun, almost never won. As for them, it was just play. Whenever we'd move, It would repeat Just as it was before. It got to where, when I'd come home, I didn't want to go back there anymore. No one knows the pain I'd feel day out and day in. Just the longing that I would have for just one Life-long friend. Then one day when I was ten I met this neighbor girl. All summer long our friendship grew 'til her parents' plan unfurled. She moved away. I painfully stayed wondering why this had to be. Until I got down in my backyard, down on my bended knee. When I asked God to fix it all, this thing He did for me. He took the pain out of my heart; from it set me free.

Before this time, I had not known If there really was a God. But since that day unto this one In pursuit of Him have I trod. Although when I was only ten, I did not know His name; I asked my parents where I should start; "We're Baptist," they proclaimed. I don't remember but just once that we'd ever been to church. But I decided I had to know; so I began my search. Then at eleven is when we moved to the country out on a farm,

Just walking distance from a Baptist Church; to go would do no harm. For the next six years, went faithfully, Wednesday, Sunday morning and night. Learned a lot of God's Word, to which I had no light.

At seventeen, when I saw a deacon curse and swear; got caught up in judging him, and fell pray to Satan's snare. The next four years, I started running around with the wrong crowd. Drinking, carousing, and doing things of which I'm not too proud. During this time, just like ole Jonah, I ran off to another land. Only to find that God was there reaching for me with His hand. Again I prayed on a hillside not ready to give in; but God was patient and so kind; and faithful to the end. Back in the States He came again; and called me by my name. Could not resist his audible voice so, I turned to Him once again. This time I knew beyond a doubt His presence is so real; and His hand was on my life; for His Spirit I could sure feel. Again I went to a Baptist Church; for this was all I knew; but soon God brought some witnesses to show me what was true. First a man from the Church of Christ showed me Acts 2:38; and said I must be baptized right if I want to see those pearly gates; but when I asked of the other part, about this Holy Ghost, he said it was not for today; then I felt, this must be a hoax. Two weeks past; and I met a man from the Assembly of God; who told me I needed the Holy Ghost to help me through life trod. But when I asked him about baptism, He said all ways are the same, so I decided to wait until More revelation came. One year went by; then almost two; and I had returned back home. Saw God do things in my life that could only have come from His throne. So again I looked at the book of Acts, chapter two, verse thirty-eight. Again, asked God to reveal the truth. This time it really came. This time as I researched His Word, I met people both left and right that had obeyed this awesome truth; and now stood there as a light. So I obeyed this Word of truth found in Acts two, verse thirty-eight. And found a friend that would stand by me all the way to those pearly gates.

Now a little more about me:

As a fifteen year old boy, I had very few friends. So, I began to spend much time with my Dad's animals and in deep thought about life. I began to express my thoughts on paper in the form of Poetry and much of my time I spent taking care of my Dad's animals I spent singing to them, making up songs then writing them down later. Although none of the music had the priveledge of being written down, I hung on the the words. Many of my poems actually started out as unwritten songs. In 1994, as an accomplished poet I had an idea. Probably not a new idea, but it was new to me. There was one of my poems that I knew had some depth to it and I knew it was as good as "Foot Prints In The Sand." What sparked this idea was walking through a new store. On their walls they displayed some decorative paper. I envisioned my poem printed upon some of that paper. So, I typed it up and then had it transferred on to one of those decorative prints. Next, I walked out on the street just a few feet away from the shop and ask a man if he would like to read my poem. He said, "Sure." I handed him a copy. He read it. Then I said, "you can have that copy for $1.00." He just reached into his pocket and pulled out a $1.00, and gave it to me. I started that afternoon with 5 copies on decorative paper. 2½ months later I had grossed $1,000.00 in *just the sale of that one poem. And that was just one-on-one direct sales. I knew that I had something. I got busy working with other poems I had written as well. In about two years, not only had I saturated my local market, but my efforts sparked other poets in my area to do the same. So, my local market played out so to speak. I knew that if I could somehow enlarge my market, I could do well just publishing and selling my writing. Another poet from Natchitoches, Louisiana heard about my business of selling my poetic works and sent me a letter enquiring of me as to how I do it. She also asked me if I could handle hers. Below is a copy of the text of the letter I sent her in return in September of 1997.*

———————

First of all, Bob's Poetry Shop is, at present, merely a business name in which I conduct business using my poetry as the basis of a product line. I've created most of my product line through using the equipment and the materials housed at local self serve printing services; and utilize the services of the same. For large orders I utilize the services of a local print shop. It all started with one poem entitled, "Two Buds," which I developed into a decorative frame-able print. Then I went door-to-door commercially selling copies of just this one print. After 2½ months, I had sold over 1,000 prints of that poem, one print at a time. That market test was a huge success; so I started developing more of my poems into the same type of product, and found that they also began to sell. Then I found I could sell laminated prints of the same. Now, I've published a book, and my newest product line is calendars and bookmarks.

Right now, I've been operating a licensed business with virtually no overhead (no building, no machine maintenance, no electric bill, etc . . .) for the last year. I've actually been selling this product line for more than four years now. Don't get me wrong. I do have plans to build a shop that would house two computers, a laminator, a binder, and sufficient storage space to operate a publication and distribution business. At present though, the physical shop is merely a dream, a goal that I'm reaching for. Right now it is just a part time business; because I also work a full time job at KFC here in Alexandria.

So far, my most profitable method of distribution has been direct sales; although I do have some books in stores such as Books-A-Million, White Steeple Books and Music, King's Emporium, and the Baptist Book Store. I am also planning on using the Internet as well. I've tried distributing the poetry of two other writers in the past; but I've found that the biggest problem I have right now is tracking. I am currently not set up to tract sales sufficiently to produce or sell another author's work. As soon as I am set up, I plan to do just that.

About 50% to 75% of my writing is inspirational or Bible-based material. With this letter I will enclose a couple of my most noted pieces. I have written tongue-twisters, romantic prose, nursery rhymes, Sunday School songs, and just for fun poems. I've been writing poetry for 27 years; and have probably lost literally thousands of pieces over the years; because I didn't really understand the gift that I had. Now that I have seen my work touch people's lives, I'm dedicated to the cause of publishing my work, hense the creation of Bob's

Poetry Shop.

I want to thank you for your interest in Bob's Poetry Shop, and I'm open to further communication with you, even meeting you, should you so desire. Perhaps as fellow poets we can share some interesting inspirational moments. I will look forward to hearing from you again soon. If you have access to email, my email address is 6ps80 at hotmail dot com (no longer active).

Since this letter, I've changed the name to Bob's Poetic Ministries, and the new email address is apoetbob@myway. com. And the book referred to in the letter is a poetry book entitled, "Let This Light So Shine".

In the meantime, I've written another book entitled "The Focused Fast," and I placed it first of all at a few local bookstores, then finally made it available online at www. bobspoeticministries.yolasite.com. While the book was in the local artist section of Books-A-Million in my area, it achieved best-seller status among the local authors. But then Books-A-Million decided to change their purchasing policy and began requiring all local authors to have an ISBN and a bar code. In the short time that it was there I sold out of my first print of this new book. Then I decided to reformat the book and try to sell it as a correspondence course. I sold about 50 more, not through mail order, but as whole binders of the complete course. So, next I reformatted again, and sold it as a half size book (5 ½ X 8 ½). So, far I've probably sold about 250 copies, including the newest CD version. Being that it is now online, I just assumed it would fly. But I now know, without the proper knowledge of how to promote the book, it won't sell there either. This book is too important (not just for me, but for the masses that could be changed by its message) to just quit and give up. I've got to find a way to get the word out to people that will not only buy the book but also read it and absorb its message. Once in a while a book comes along that has the power to change lives. And, believe me, this is one of those books. I've seen it work in people's lives already. One of the ladies that I ask to proof read the book told me that each paragraph she read sent her to her knees weeping. She had to pray through each paragraph. Now, I know that it won't affect everyone like that; but I'm sure there are others that will be affected that way.

Finally, I uploaded several books online that are presently for sale at the following sites: www.bobspoeticministries. yolasite.com; www.poetbob.com; www.poetbob.ws; www. poetbobsgiftsuperstore.com including a four volume set of my Inspirational poetry entitled "Becoming". If you would like to be encouraged, strengthened, uplifted, or edified in anyway, take some time and visit my bookstores and review my books.

More Recently, I moved to the Paris, Tennessee area where I have spent much more time on the publishing end of my writing. And now, I have entered into this working relationship with PageTurner, Press and Media publishing to bring you one new book, Becoming!: A Lifetime of Prose.

My Family Background

Born December 19th, 1954, the 5th of seven children of Elmo & Emma McGlothlin, I grew up in the Central Louisiana area. I attended Carter C. Raymond Elementary for about 6 months at the age of 5, then the family moved to Alexandria where I attended Cherokee Elementary for 6 months. Then they started me over in the 1st grade again at Horseshoe Elementery for 5 years. We then moved out to the Latania community just outside of Lecompte, Louisiana where I attended Poland High School (at that time a 1-12 school) for the remainder of my basic education. Then I went 1 symester to LSU at Alexandria, LA, followed by 3 years and 2 months in the USAF. When I got out of the military, I took 1 symester at Louisiana College in Pineville. But due to a radical change in my life, I dropped out of college altogether to pursue a brave new goal in life, the Will of God. That radical change was an experience most call "The Born Again Experience". Just before I moved to Tennessee, my parents needed some help, so I took off 5 years to be their caretaker. In the middle of that 5 years, we moved my parents and myself up here to Tennessee. After their passing, I got work up here.

Lightning Source UK Ltd.
Milton Keynes UK
UKHW04f0853040918
328299UK00001B/73/P